Holding the Moment

MID-AMERICA AT MID-CENTURY

Holding the Moment

MID-AMERICA AT MID-CENTURY

Text and photographs by DON ULTANG

Iowa State University Press / Ames

The author and the publisher wish to acknowledge the
cooperation of the *Des Moines Register,* where many of
these photographs first appeared.

©1991 Iowa State University Press, Ames, Iowa 50010

Manufactured in the United States of America
∞ This book is printed on acid-free paper.

First edition, 1991

Library of Congress Cataloging-in-Publication Data

Ultang, Don.
    Holding the moment : mid-America at mid-century / text and photographs by Don Ultang. – 1st ed.
      p. cm.
    Includes index.
    ISBN 0-8138-1019-1 (alk. paper). – ISBN 0-8138-1018-3 (pbk.: alk. paper)
    1. Middle West – Social life and customs – Pictorial works. 2. Middle West – Description and
travel – Views. 3. Photojournalism – Middle West – History – 20th century.   I. Title.
F354.U44 1991
977 – dc20   90-48684

To the memory of my parents
Martin Oliver Ultang
Elida Skuldt Ultang

And to my daughters
Linda, Caroline, and Joanne

Contents

Foreword *by Clark Mollenhoff*   ix

Preface   xi

Acknowledgments   xiv

1 The Passing Era   3

Gallery I   11

2 Low and Fast   43

Gallery II   59

3 Journalism and the Unobtrusive Camera   103

Gallery III   131

Endnote   187

Index   189

About the author   193

Foreword

The photographs and prose in Don Ultang's book represent a beautifully illustrated nostalgic look at the golden era of photojournalism.

From his vantage point as staff photographer and pilot for the *Des Moines Register* and *Tribune,* Don Ultang ranged across the upper midwest to record historic as well as the mundane activities of children, farmers, athletes and businessmen and women of the thirties, forties and fifties.

Ultang's artistry with a camera is matched with a poetic feel for words in explaining the photographs with relevant and effective research that gives a fine historic perspective to the book. The story behind the photographs is blended with material on Ultang's personal life and development as a great photojournalist to give the reader a short history of the development of photojournalism in newspapers and magazines.

I flew with Don Ultang on a number of joint photographic and news story assignments in the late 1940s, and at an early stage recognized the great facility he had in aerial photography in his skillful coordination of the controls of the plane and the control over the shutter of the camera to catch just the right angle and right lighting. I also had an early recognition of the thought and study he put into his work to bring an artistry to what would otherwise have been routine picture assignments. His explanatory manuscript has a poetry and well-researched historic perspective that brings greater meaning to his pictures.

Anyone born and reared in Iowa or in the upper-midwest—or interested in the photographic artistry of the twentieth century—will find pure pleasure in the nostalgic review of the life work of this highly talented Pulitzer Prize–winning photojournalist.

CLARK MOLLENHOFF

Preface

Aphotojournalist is a recorder of history, a visual scribe whose images document the changing times. The emergence of great public personalities, the eruption of the calamitous forces of nature, the subtle but profound alterations in the patterns of American life—each event marks the passing of time. Where the remote and secluded Passionist monastery stood, a mall and its trendy shops compete for buyers' attention. Montana and the Dakotas now quarrel with Iowa over the flow of the Missouri River waters that through the fifties raged unchecked each spring. The Iron Curtain of Winston Churchill lifted as the Berlin Wall crumbled. And corn shocks, snow blanketed sentinels of the rural winter scene, disappeared with the advent of giant grain combines. For fifty years I have recorded such changes in my photographs. In *Holding the Moment,* I look back at all that appeared before the lens of my camera during the critical decades of the 1930s, the 1940s, and the 1950s.

I consider myself fortunate to have been part of some of the great changes of the twentieth century, though I didn't set out to do so. In the days just before World War II, while a student at the University of Iowa and a freelance photographer, or learning to be one, events at the university shaped the course of my professional career. A number of examples come to mind.

The university founded a group of bag pipers, the Scottish Highlanders, who became famous for their performances at halftime at the Iowa football games. My first photograph in a major national magazine was a 1939 full-page photograph in *The American Magazine,* showing the leader of the Highlanders in full Scottish regalia.

A fellow student and friend of mine at Iowa, Henry Felsen (later a nationally known fiction writer) had a brother who came back from the

Spanish Civil War having lost a leg fighting General Franco. I photographed his brother for the *Cedar Rapids Gazette* when he visited Iowa City.

When Dr. Eddie Anderson came to the University of Iowa to rebuild the football program my photographs of his night arrival at the Rock Island railroad train station and the greeting given him by staff members of the university's athletic department were displayed in both the *Des Moines Register* and the *Cedar Rapids Gazette.* Dr. Anderson went on to develop the famous 1939 Big Ten football team properly called the Ironmen. Nile Kinnick, leader of the Ironmen and an Adel, Iowa, youth, skilled both athletically and academically, was in one of my classes that year, the same year he became an All-American quarterback and a Heisman Trophy winner; the University of Iowa football stadium is today named in his honor. Tragically, he would die early in the war when he was forced to ditch his Navy fighter plane at sea.

I had little recognition of the forces at work that would lead to World War II and, following the war, the many cultural and economic changes that would alter our century irrevocably. I didn't know I would record many of these changes, one way or another, but as it turned out a place on the photographic staff of one of America's leading newspapers was ideal. The fact that I could live in Iowa, always my home, made it even more desirable.

After World War II our country moved from building tanks and bombers, planting victory gardens, and saving rolls of string to constructing new factories and schools and producing enough food to feed a growing nation. While Americans struggled with postwar problems, in mid-America nature maintained its continuing assaults in the form of blizzards, thunderstorms, tornadoes, and dust storms, many of which reached record-breaking proportions. All this offered dramatic and powerful material for my camera.

During the forties and fifties, photography as an art form—debated at length in photographic journals and rejected outright in many conservative art circles—grew in my consciousness. While developing a sense of what I wanted to do as I recorded history in passing—as well as a sense of the opportunity I had to inform and entertain with photographs of lasting quality—I came to the belief that photojournalism was the most satisfying, and perhaps demanding, vehicle for one who wanted to deal with reality and to apply whatever measure of artistry possible. I also learned that photojournalists must improvise regularly. Conceptualization, in the sense Ansel Adams used the term, was not our privilege. I always felt I understood immediately the potential of a photographic situation and continued to search until the potential was met.

Henri Cartier-Bresson reinforced my thoughts about photojournalism. In the preface of his famous book, *The Decisive Moment,* he remarked: "To me, photography is the simultaneous recognition, in a fraction of a second, of the significance of an event as well as of a precise organization of forms which give that event its proper expression.

"For me, content cannot be separated from form. By form, I mean a rigorous organization of the interplay of surfaces, lines and values. It is in this organization alone that our conceptions and emotions become concrete and communicable. In photography, visual organization can stem only from a developed instinct."

The photographs of Alfred Stieglitz, founder of the turn-of-the-century Photo-Secession group, moved me significantly; they offered light and shadow, form and tonal range in a compelling, profound manner. Stieglitz stated, "What is of greatest importance is to hold a moment, to record something so completely that those who see it will relive an equivalent of what has been experienced." This expressed my feelings accurately.

If the forties and fifties comprised the golden age of newspapers and general circulation magazines, then they were also the golden age of photojournalism. My work at the *Des Moines Register* and *Tribune* brought me in contact with a variety of subjects and a full range of assignments. One day the activity would be a flight to cover a presidential campaign, the next day a flight to the Iowa State penitentiary at Fort Madison to cover an inmate-turned-autobiographer. Then, a few days later, a picture story would materialize on the leading lady at the Des Moines Little Theater.

Day after day I worked to record, to the best of my ability, images of events—some dramatic, others more prosaic—and the people involved in them. I offer them here as visual records of the history of mid-America in the middle of the twentieth century—to hold the moment and here and there capture a permanent image, forging a link to the present.

Acknowledgments

I owe much to many but especially to the following:

My wife, Elizabeth Kasten-Ultang, whose encouragement led to the resurrection of old prints and negatives stored and forgotten; Bill Shaefer and Ron Darge, both instrumental in organizing the retrospective exhibit that became the basis for the book; my editor, Bill Silag, a constant and enthusiastic source of support; and Veda Richards Ultang, who for forty-five years of married life, until her death in 1985, lived with a roaming photojournalist and aviator.

In addition, Kenneth MacDonald, Bernard Mercer, and Martin Krakauer, all helpful at major turning points in my life.

And Bob Garmon, aviation mechanic and friend, whose skills kept our aircraft airborne during critical times.

Holding the Moment

MID-AMERICA AT MID-CENTURY

1

The Passing Era

The decade of the 1930s embraced an economic depression so overwhelming to America's millions it is still referred to as the Great Depression. As the searing winds spawned the Dust Bowl—so vividly depicted in John Steinbeck's *The Grapes of Wrath*—gigantic federal aid programs such as the National Recovery Act, the Civilian Conservation Corps, and the Works Progress Administration were launched to pull the nation out of the economic mire.

In Iowa, the thirties were important years of social change, some of it prompted by the Depression and some of it the result of a more gradual process of technical advance. Roads were paved at an increasing rate, and none too soon. I remember as a boy taking an automobile trip from Fort Dodge to Cedar Rapids with my father and mother, who found a short detour in Tama County on the coast to coast Lincoln Highway to be a mud hole. Our touring sedan, a 1924 Baby Grand Chevrolet, had a cloth top and removable isinglass side curtains to protect passengers from the rain, but even the car's great road clearance found mud up to the running boards too much to handle.

Shoes and socks removed, trousers rolled above his knees and dress shirt above his elbows, my father dug his lean arms into the wet clay between the wooden spokes and under the fenders—to no avail. A nearby farmer and his ready team of mules finally pulled us from the mud hole. We slept overnight in the upstairs spare bedroom of the railroad station-master at Gladstone, Iowa, in a house adjacent to the railroad tracks and still standing close to Highway 30.

Understandably, Iowans voted to build all-weather farm-to-market roads, and the federal highways improved during the thirties and especially following World War II. During Dwight D. Eisenhower's administration in the fifties, the interstate highway system would begin.

But in the thirties commerce relied less heavily on the roadways than it does now. First-class mail raced across the nation on steel rails and in specially equipped U.S. Mail cars. Express mail trains—thundering through small towns with a window-rattling, roaring crescendo, belching smoke and showers of fine, hot cinders—snatched up heavy canvas mail bags left hanging within reach of a long arm extending from the mail car. Inside, mail clerks sorted letters and packages while the train pounded and whistled its way between major stops, all across the land.

Commercial aviation, stimulated in the thirties by government subsidies to airlines, grew rapidly. The twin-engine DC-3 and its military counterpart, the C-47, the personnel and cargo workhorses of World War II, had been developed a decade earlier. Only a few years earlier (1927), Lindbergh flew, alone and without autopilot across the Atlantic—over thirty-three hours in his single engine monoplane—and changed the world's view of aviation. This was a major historic event. My parents drove from Fort Dodge to Des Moines in our black open-sided touring sedan to see Lindbergh land the *Spirit of St. Louis* on a grass field northeast of the city. The people there became excited as the small speck on the horizon grew larger, and a great cheer rose from the crowd as the Ryan-built aircraft touched down.

Lindbergh's solo flight forecast the dependability of aircraft of the future, and technical developments presaged a new era in automotive transport as well. Touring cars were to give way to automobiles with steel bodies, genuine glass in the side windows, hydraulic brakes, and eventually heating and air conditioning for passenger comfort. World War II accelerated aircraft and automotive development, but the direction of change was evident in the thirties.

Technical progress was changing the way people lived in other ways too. In the countryside, rural electrification was well under way when the United States entered the war.

By the end of the forties, most of rural America had benefited by the Rural Electrification Administration (REA) program. This period also saw the growing rise of the gasoline tractor, first equipped with steel-bladed wheels rather than rubber tires. The internal combustion engine forced the demise of steam-powered tractors as well as the use of horses and mules, forever changing the way much farm work was done. Putting up hay, for example. Great hay mows had been built into most of the early barns in the upper middle west; fierce winters demanded forage for cattle and horses for half of the year or more. Loose hay was laboriously swung by ropes and pulleys into a large opening on the upper face of the barn. The power was animal power–horses, mules, and men. After the thirties, large barns with hay mows were no longer built, and forage is now baled or put up as silage.

Conveniences such as electricity and running water were already established in the cities. The General Electric Monitor refrigerator, named after the U.S.S. *Monitor,* ironclad warship of Civil War fame with its solitary revolving gun turret mounted in the center of a flat deck, became well-known because of the large, look-alike compressor turret placed conspiciously on top of the white refrigerator; the circular dome became a symbol of domestic affluence. Horse-drawn ice wagons–and ice cards in the front window indicating the day's required amount for the ice box–were gradually taken from service. The muscular figure of an ice man with huge iron tongs, a tool with sharply pointed pinchers designed to grasp and hold fifty pounds of ice on a man's leather-padded back, disappeared from the tree-lined residential streets. Children could no longer grab cooling slivers of ice on a hot summer day. Milk wagons, drawn by horses who knew the route as well as the delivery man, were replaced by trucks. When home delivery of milk disappeared, our cold winters could no longer freeze bottles of milk and force the cream with bottle cap attached an inch into the freezing morning air. Quart milk bottles–cream at the top and milk at the bottom–were still common a number of years after World War II, but they too would eventually fall out of fashion.

Although street cars and interurbans continued to run during and after the war, the growing use of automobiles and buses for our basic transportation needs was under way. Some cities compromised with curbliners, giant buses fueled by electric power from an overhead trolley line. These too eventually gave way to the fossil fuel buses. Our natural gas supply was yet to be fully tapped, and coal furnaces were still common in homes. Converting the coal furnace by the installation of an oil burning heating unit became common in the thirties.

Television and computers were yet to come, but the electronic revolution had begun. I can recall, as a seven-year old living in Fort Dodge, standing on the sidewalk outside a Central Avenue cigar store, listening to parts of the first Dempsey-Tunney fight. Our first home radio–an Atwater Kent with three independent tuning dials, causing great squawks until properly aligned—brought in KDKA-Pittsburgh with clarity and strength. Local stations were weak and not numerous. But the airways, as the spectrum of frequencies was then called, did not stay uncluttered long. Great sporting events of the twenties aided radio's universal acceptance in American homes and helped it become the communication medium of the thirties and forties. Nothing better symbolized its eventual importance than Franklin Delano Roosevelt's "fireside chats," which gave hope to America at the depth of the Depression and throughout the war years.

A sophomore in the fall of 1936, I entered the School of Journalism at the University of Iowa. Frank Luther Mott, later director of the journalism program at the University of Missouri, was the director at Iowa. Reporting was the primary course, and the news photography course was minimal. Photography was not to be thrust upon me until some months later. My experience as a reporter on the *Daily Iowan*—with Merle Miller (later the author of *Island 49, Plain Speaking,* and other well-received books) as city editor—provided my first contact with working journalism. It was a new and exciting world.

Bob Sherwood and Mary Burke, two journalism students putting themselves through school as stringers for various newspapers, needed a responsible, motivated news photographer, and somehow we found one another. During my last two years at Iowa, Sherwood and Burke supplied news leads, and I tried to cover every happening in Iowa City and Johnson County. The *Cedar Rapids Gazette,* the *Davenport Times,* and the *Omaha World-Herald* helped fill my stringbook with clippings, as did the *Des Moines Register* sports department. The payment was one dollar for each published photograph—and an "Ultang Photo" credit.

The standard photographic equipment of the day, heavy and cumbersome compared to today's offerings, was not appealing to me. The then-new 35mm equipment offered a lightweight alternative, but my first effort to experience the artistic freedom of a 35mm camera ended in failure. The camera, bought in 1937, was a used Retina, an ingenious folding unit with a miniature leather bellows, an excellent Schneider-Xenar F:3.5 lens, and a Compur shutter. This imported camera was Eastman Kodak's response to the German-built 35mm Leica introduced a few years earlier and immediately established as the world's leading 35mm camera. (The only person I knew who owned a Leica was a Cedar Rapids physician who took very few photographs but in those Depression days knew the pleasure of possessing the ultimate in camera hardware.) To my dismay, every roll of film used in the Retina produced thin scratch lines the full length of the film. The struggle with these blemishes on the film surface led me to a more standard film size. Rolleiflex, the famous twin-lens reflex, was expensive, and I settled for its less costly companion, the Rolleicord. This camera carried me into the early stages of journalistic photography.

The flash gun mounted on my Rolleicord was synchronized mechanically to the opening and closing of the shutter by a Kalart spring device and cable release, which had to be cocked for each exposure just as the shutter had to be cocked. With much care and understanding, the Kalart synchronizer could be made to work most of the time.

The era of built-in, automatic electronic flash still lay ahead. Flash bulbs, filled with aluminum foil, were as large as a man's fist, producing immense amounts of light and often leaving a seared, raw hand when the bulb ignited while being pressed into the flash gun socket. Only a few years earlier flash powder was still in use. The powder, in an elongated tray held in one hand above the photographer's head and ignited by firing a cap, flared abruptly with a loud *whump!* and much smoke—eventually mantling fine, gray ash over the photographer and his subjects. Thus, I was the beneficiary of some measure of progress.

Kodachrome transparency color film was available, but practical negative color film was not produced for another thirty or forty years. Later I was to learn that Eastman Kodak had first marketed Kodachrome only two years earlier (1935) after Leopold Mannes and Leopold Godowsky, two professional musicians who were also amateur photographers and chemists, surprised the photographic world with their new color process. Kodachrome's competition was negligible. Dufaycolor from France, offering home processing, was an unsatisfactory option. Eastman Kodak had no serious competition and, despite its slow emulsion speed (ASA 10), Kodachrome for many years was the only desirable color emulsion.

Although a few national magazines occasionally printed color, photography in general and photojournalism in particular was a black and white medium and continued so for another two decades. Photographs offering garish crimsons and strong yellows constantly stated that color

was new and daring, and predictable static posing was the style. There-
fore black and white remained dominant and gave the era its look. For
example, the photographs in the Harry S. Truman Library in Independence, Missouri, tracing his career until he died in 1972, offer no color
images. Eleven years after Truman's death, my youngest grandson, Jedd,
six years old at the time, studied the many images, turned to his parents,
and asked, "Did all the world used to be black and white?"

In Iowa City in the late thirties, my contribution to the photographic
record began. The subject matter was varied and challenging to a young
photographer. For example, at the university, Dr. Eddie Anderson became the focal point for a winning football program. Ice storms knocked
down country power lines. The Amish lumber yard in Kalona burned to
the ground, and Old Capitol, simple and beautiful, lent its classic lines to
my eye. Whatever was of interest was material for my camera lens.

But graduation day in 1939 left me a vocational orphan. Short on
journalism credits at the end of my third year, an economics major appeared to be the best alternative. However, a would-be photojournalist
certainly didn't fit into the field of economics. And the school of journalism didn't have a great responsibility to help find a job for an economics
major and a fallen-away journalism student. (Dr. Mott, as director at the
University of Missouri, eventually invited me to speak on the same
journalism program as Alfred Eisenstaedt of *Life,* the father of modern
photojournalism, but that would be fifteen years later.)

Roy Hardendorf, a Cedar Rapids camera shop owner, came to my
rescue by hiring me as a flunky in his camera shop darkroom. Sitting in
the greenish-yellow light from a Wratten OA filter hanging in the shad-
owy room, head cocked sideways to miss the smoke curling from the wet
and droopy cigarette always stuck at the corner of his mouth, he operated
an aged Jumbo printer all day long and taught me the fine points of
making and processing prints properly. Tait Cummins, *Cedar Rapids Gazette* sports editor, agreed to try my idea of getting better football coverage at the University of Iowa Big Ten games for his Sunday sports
page. The *Gazette* had a contract with Dan Hunter, local pilot and airport
operator, and one Saturday I found myself on my first flight to cover a Big
Ten football game—all of the thirty miles from Cedar Rapids to Iowa City.
Nile Kinnick and Iowa's renowned Ironmen, all playing both offense and
defense on Iowa's football team, made the fall of 1939 a challenging and
rewarding autumn.

The *Gazette* had no staff photographer in 1939, and my enthusiasm prompted me to make the paper a proposal. Finding editor Verne Marshall in his office, I tried to open the subject. Marshall, a strong-willed, nationally recognized figure in Charles Lindbergh's "America First" effort to keep the United States out of the war just started in Europe, shouted and waved me out of his office doorway. He had no time for, nor interest in, such a discussion.

The winter was bleak, and the coming of 1940 gave little promise. M.A. Aasgaard, owner and publisher of the *Lake Mills Graphic,* even today one of Iowa's finest small-town papers, wanted a combination portrait and commercial photographer in his community. In the dead of winter, a town of no more than two thousand people near the Iowa-Minnesota border had no appeal for a journalistically motivated photographer. But a chance comment by a traveling photo products man brought the information to Cedar Rapids that the *Des Moines Register* and *Tribune* had been looking for a staff replacement for some time. An appointment arranged, my tattered and ragged stringbook in hand, I drove to Des Moines and a few weeks after my interview was on a newspaper photographic staff recognized to be one of the best in the nation and happy to be issued a hand-me-down Speed Graphic with a Heiland flash gun and ten cut film holders.

Not many years earlier, the staff, led by chief photographer George Yates, had used 5 × 7 Folmer-Graflex cameras and often disrupted news coverage with clouds of smoke and the black residue resulting from the use of flash powder. The transition to 35mm cameras and a changing photojournalistic philosophy was still to come.

The Passing Era *Gallery I*

The photographs in the following group are the strongest and most significant of those I took from the late thirties through the immediate post-war period. They do not represent all the social and economic activities of this critical period; rather they should be viewed as a sampling of the world that met one photographer's eye.

Seventh and Locust, Des Moines, 1941. Four days after
the bombing of Pearl Harbor, "WAR" in the newspaper
headlines, and a gentle, pre-Christmas snowfall.

Old Capitol, Iowa City, 1938.

Oat mill, Cedar Rapids, 1938.

Southeast bottoms, Des Moines, 1941.

Old man in church, 1941. >

Haying scenes, Linn County, 1938.

March 1, farmers' annual moving day, 1938.

Corn husking, 1940.

Telephone central, Truro, 1946.

Ironmen leaders. University of Iowa football coach Eddie
Anderson and Nile Kinnick address a student rally at Old
Capitol, 1938. Also, Kinnick, All-American and 1939
Heisman Trophy winner, visits with Sally Tubbs, daughter
of coach Irl Tubbs, 1939 (above, right).

Girls' basketball state championship game—Wiota vs.
Clutier, 1942.

World War II victory garden, 1942.

Jitterbug contest on Center Street, 1940.

Cloris Leachman, Miss Chicago, 1946. Also, Cloris at home with sisters Claiborne and Mary.

Coal smog over Des Moines, 1940.

Railroad yard, 1940.

Burlington railroad shops, 1946.

At the railroad station, school children wave farewell to
the final train out of Humeston, Iowa, 1940.

The early days of television starred "Kookla, Fran and Ollie," a children's show watched by many adults. It had warmth, humor and fantasy. Kookla and Ollie were puppets, the former a Punch and Judy character and Ollie, a friendly alligator. Fran Allison was an attractive, charming talking-head placed within inches of the right side of the puppet set. And she made Kookla and Ollie come to life. America loved all three when Fran Allison came to visit her hometown of Waterloo, Iowa. On a routine assignment I flew there to get photographs for the *Register*. Kookla and Ollie failed to make an appearance, but Fran Allison helped me capture on film a moment of exuberance. Although steam locomotives were disappearing and automobiles with kerosene head lamps were no longer on the road, the organizers of her homecoming had a surprise—a race between a steam engine, full size, and a 1908 Oldsmobile.

An enthusiastic crowd jammed the small space between the old downtown train depot and warehouse buildings across from the finish line. A proper vantage point for a photograph had to be high and clear of the heads of onlookers. After a long wait, the struggling, pounding locomotive could be heard. Smoke and haze hid the engine, and no evidence of an antique automobile could be seen or heard. At the last second the giant bulk of the steam engine caught up with the smoke and roar it was producing. Bursting through the gray curtain of smoke and haze, the turn-of-the-century Oldsmobile raced along side the roaring engine. Goggles in place, the driver strained to force his antique to victory. Seated to his left in a wonderful Gibson Girl outfit, duster included, holding onto the floppy brim of her hat with one hand and the seat with the other was Fran Allison. She loved every second, as the two vehicles roared to the finish line. Kookla and Ollie would have been happy for their friend.

Home town celebration for Waterloo's Fran Allison of
television's "Kookla, Fran, and Ollie," 1954.

Old coal tipple, Appanoose County, 1946.

Three men and a cat, 1941.

Confidentially, at the Polk County Courthouse, 1942.

2

Low and Fast

My first experience with aerial photography came in 1941 – prior to going into the Navy – while learning to fly in the Civilian Pilot Training Program. Congress funded the CPT program in an effort to build a good supply of potential military pilots in the event the war was thrust upon us. I knew little about Congressional expectations, but I knew I wanted to learn to fly.

The training consisted of two courses. The first developed the skills to get a private pilot's license, including a requirement that all pilots learn to spin the aircraft and recover from the spin. Nothing could seem more demanding than a two-turn precision spin, and thus the decision to take the second course, acrobatics, was not difficult to make. As my schedule at the *Register* left my mornings free, that time could be spent learning to perform loops, slow rolls and snap rolls, and improving my skills in turns at low altitude.

The editor of our Sunday Rotogravure section, Carl Gartner, agreed to a picture story on the Civilian Pilot Training Program. The flying service helped get all of the trainees together. I took the basic photographs of airplanes taking off, of starting engines by physically grasping the propeller and pulling it through by hand, and of ground school classes on aerodynamics, engines, meteorology, and navigation. But I was still without a dramatic key photograph, one with impact and strong visual appeal.

In 1941, aerobatics meant open cockpit aircraft, leather helmets and goggles and heads hanging upside down in the slip stream. Instructor and student, in separate and tandem cockpits, kept from falling out by use of a safety belt. Occasionally a student failed to tighten the safety belt properly and got a surprise when he dropped three inches onto the safety belt as the aircraft rolled onto its back. With this sensation in mind, I shot a photograph of an aerobatic trainee in normal flight taken from an inverted plane. The instructor's head in the foreground – hanging upside down where the sky and ground met – would allow the newspaper reader a sense of being in a rolling aircraft.

Hanging from an open cockpit over rolling hills and fields of corn, 1941.

Concerned that the camera might be dropped accidently from the inverted plane, I looped a rope through the leather camera grip and through the belt on my trousers. The camera did feel extraordinarily heavy, and handling loose film holders and dark slides while upside down was a problem, but nothing was lost to the ground below. The upside-down photograph became the lead image in the CPT picture story.

War rallies were common in 1942, and one of these gave me additional experience in aerial photography. An Army Air Corps detachment (not Air Force until later in the war) was the main attraction at a rally in Drake University football stadium. The Air Corps pilot explained he would make a simulated dive-bombing run on the tents at the war show bivouac in the open fields at what is now Fifty-fourth Street and Franklin Avenue in Des Moines. The open rear cockpit, normally the machine gunner's seat, was the only place for a photographer.

At dusk we made the dive-bombing run at the bivouac area. As we climbed sharply skyward following the run, the rear gunner's seat gave me a wonderful view of the regular rows of army tents with the tail of the aircraft framing the image. After total nightfall, we repeated this run by diving through the crowded Drake Stadium. The darkness prevented a photograph, but the bivouac area image and a number of air-to-air formation photographs made a fine layout in the *Tribune,* our afternoon paper.

Limited though my pre-war experience was, it made me confident that I could take dramatic aerial photographs. When the opportunity arose after the war, my photographic techniques worked well.

Don Ultang, Navy flight instructor, 1943.

When I came out of military service in January 1946, I came back to a Des Moines outwardly changed very little. Fort Des Moines had been the headquarters of the Women's Auxiliary Corps (WACs), and a munitions plant had been built north of Des Moines at Ankeny. Commercial activity at Firestone, Armstrong, and John Deere Tractor replaced military production. Generally, most things looked familiar.

Des Moines still had passenger train service, only a few DC-3's flew the airline routes, and concrete for the interstate highway system would not be poured for another decade. In common with most other cities in America, we used coal to fuel our industry and our homes. The average Iowa farm was relatively small, a few families still getting along on 120 acres. Farmers continued to alter their corn acreage with oats and rotation pasture over a three- to five-year period, although some farmers were trying out soybeans. Hay was put up in hay mows, and a manure spreader was still an important farm implement.

Harry S. Truman was president. When he campaigned in 1952 I flew the *Des Moines Register* and *Tribune* plane to what was then known as the Tri-Cities (Davenport, Rock Island, and Moline) in order to photograph Truman speaking from the rear platform of his campaign train as he whistle stopped through mid-America. I happened to be the pilot of a newspaper plane for many reasons, a major one being the effect World War II had on the direction my life took.

The Civilian Pilot Training courses, taken while working as a staff photographer for the Des Moines papers, had led to my becoming a naval aviator, and I had spent the war as a flight instructor for the Navy. The hundreds of hours of low altitude flight while training new Navy pilots were invaluable to me as a pilot-photographer. The experience I gained kept me from flying into the ground while intent on photographing a train wreck or a snowbound truck as my airplane skimmed two hundred feet over the tree tops. Further, I had become very comfortable close to the ground as long as the aircraft remained well above stalling speed during my photographic passes. Those hours in the air as a Navy flight instructor also gave me the credentials to help convince Kenneth MacDonald (the *Register* editor who fortunately had become knowledgeable about naval aviation while serving as an officer at the same time I was an officer and an instructor) that I could successfully combine the two roles of photographer and pilot. He remained a positive force behind the editorial flight operation throughout the eventful years between 1946 and 1959.

One of the changes the war had made was in the design of aircraft, and we were now able to find fast and maneuverable single-engine aircraft. In these planes for the next decade we roamed mid-America in search of stories and photographs. Although a two-place, 125 h.p. Globe Swift was a good aircraft for the first few years of the editorial flight operation, we purchased our first 170-mile-per-hour aircraft, a Beechcraft Bonanza, in 1949. At that time it cruised ten miles an hour faster than the standard aircraft for the airlines, the venerable DC-3. We could fly long distances, and we could land in small fields. Covering the state of Iowa was our primary goal, but all surrounding states now became legitimate territory. We covered football games as far away as Stillwater, Oklahoma (where we garnered a Pulitzer Prize for the newspaper) and Pittsburgh, Pennsylvania. (The games were often still in progress during a portion of our return flights.) When the Iowa angle was sufficiently strong, we reached out to the northwest as far as the Dakotas and Montana and to the southwest into the Rio Grande valley of Texas. When two Des Moines Boy Scouts were lost for a number of days in the Arizona desert, we were there. One year we followed the Iowa Flying Farmers to Monterrey, Mexico.

Until the mid-fifties the *Register*'s aircraft was busy each spring covering devastating floods on the Des Moines River or the muddy Missouri River. Later, of course, flood control projects financed by federal funds slowly brought these damaging waters under control. But in 1952 and 1954 the overflowing Missouri maintained its flood stage as it passed southward along the border between Nebraska and Iowa for such a long period that each day for more than a week it was my assignment to roam the broad expanse for dramatic photographs.

Although in these post-war years the aircraft industry tooled up in the hope of putting a small plane in every garage in America, the fact is there were not many aircraft in the skies; the freedom to come and go, to fly as you please, was not hindered by many regulations. The general rule about low level flying was to the effect that you could not fly so low as to endanger persons or property. This left much to the judgment of the pilot, allowing me to fly close enough to get strong images.

The first post-war attention I received as a photographer came in September 1947 when *Life* carried a full-page aerial photograph of mine.

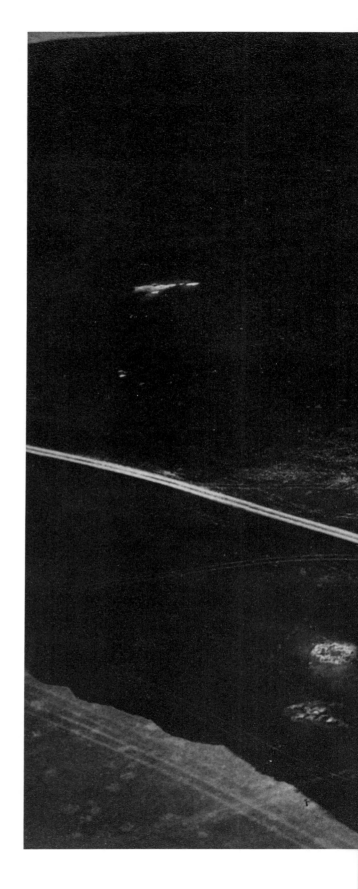

Blackened prairie, South Dakota, 1947. This photograph
was exhibited at the New York Museum of Modern Art in
Edward Steichen's *The Exact Instant,* representing "the
greatest photographs taken in the last 100 years." Also,
U.S. Camera Annual 1949 and *Photography Annual 1954.*

An assignment from the *Register*'s editors to cover a gigantic prairie fire in the middle of South Dakota had sent me and our plane winging north-west. As this was open range land without many natural navigational landmarks, my first problem was to find the prairie fire with the general directions I had been given. My mind was full of thoughts about what I would find. Getting an image of more than a dense cloud of smoke was my second and very real concern. Flames on the leading edge of a prairie fire would not show clearly in an aerial photograph. I continued to specu-late as the aircraft droned across the northeast corner of Nebraska and on course over the ranch land of South Dakota. An ominous black pall finally cloaked the far horizon. After a general survey, a ranch house, threatened by the flames, appeared below me. Square miles of burned, blackened prairie grass were visible to the south and west of my position in the air. Still, I continued my search for a more dramatic situation.

In the distance, growing more distinct as the plane closed in, a one-room schoolhouse gradually appeared. Spared by the flames as the prairie burned its way northward during the night, the white schoolhouse looked like a jewel on black velvet, untouched because local ranchers had the wisdom to plow a large square of earth around the small building, protect-ing it from the all-consuming fire. From my vantage point three-hundred feet above, the angles of the plowed earth and the white wagon wheel trails through the blackened grass made a fine image. I circled two or three times, taking a photograph from a different perspective each pass. With our first-edition deadline my next concern, firmly I banked the plane toward the southeast to head back to Des Moines.

The drama of the subject and the interesting composition of the image were all I could have hoped for. The pictures made a strong layout in the morning *Register*—strong enough that the schoolhouse photograph was sent out as a wire photo and used nationwide. That in itself was routine, but much to my surprise the next issue of *Life* featured my blackened prairie schoolhouse as a full-page photograph. To my dismay the credit line was "INT." In addition, *Life* paid space rates, which went to International. I protested to *Life,* but was told by *Life*'s editors that the only way I could have received credit and payment was to have mailed a print directly to *Life.* The lesson was learned: each Friday in the future, if I had particularly interesting material, I made certain *Life* got a copy directly.

One of the photographs I took of the little white schoolhouse, "Blackened Prairie," was exhibited in the New York Museum of Modern Art by Edward Steichen, then photography curator at the museum, who organized an exhibit entitled *The Exact Instant,* celebrating one hundred years of American photography. Later the "Blackened Prairie" hung in the *Subjektive Fotografie* exhibit in Saarbrucken, West Germany. This was not the same photograph as sent to *Life* over the wire, as the exhibit photograph included much of the surrounding blackened grassland. In this view, the white schoolhouse floats on a sea of blackness.

A few months after flying to the South Dakota fire, I received a telegram from *Life* in New York offering congratulations on two photographs I had sent them. It was 1948, and spring had come to Iowa in its usual blustery mix of wind and rain. My photographs told a story about the changing of the seasons from a new and different perspective and in a way that had strong eye appeal. One was of a horse-drawn farm wagon, loaded with family members of all ages, escaping flood waters. The other was a contour plowing scene, farm house in the distance, with the curving lines made by the plowman, and the late afternoon sun offering a rare view of an Iowa farmer at work. *Life* used the two large aerial photographs, on facing pages, under the heading "Spring Comes to Iowa."

Two full-page photographs in a single spread in *Life* was more good fortune than I had thought possible. Even *Life* staffers rarely had that experience.

The first half of "Spring Comes to Iowa" was photographed late in the day on a return flight from eastern Iowa in March, with a strong northwest wind gusting to thirty or forty miles an hour. With the low afternoon light casting deep shadows across the furrows of black earth, I made five or six passes over this contour plowing scene near Montezuma, Iowa. Each turn over the target area had to be timed with the farmer's steady, constant progress as the furrows opened in great looping curves. But the staggering, turbulent wind made each pass a struggle to hold the right flight path and properly control the aircraft near the ground. Even normal wing-level flight was uncomfortable; the extremely steep bank needed to check wind drift was startling. On the first pass, the near-gale winds blew the aircraft well beyond the plowman and the hillside contours, and I was too far away to warrant a photograph. Four passes later, each an improvement, I precisely judged the progress of the tractor and plow, the contour lines on the sloping farm land, the position of distant farm buildings—and the savage wind.

Spring comes to Iowa, 1948. *Life* published each
photograph on a full page and stated, "Once again the
swollen rivers flooded farm houses and lapped across the
highways in a last defiant gesture. And once again on

higher ground the farmers were at work contour plowing
their fields, the land was as good as ever and crops would
be fine if summer would only fulfill the abundant promise
of spring." Also, *U.S. Camera Annual 1949.*

Just right! When I heard the curtain shutter thump to its close I knew a strong, telling image had been captured. My passenger, a *Register* reporter, was airsick. I was physically exhausted. With feelings of accomplishment and relief, I rolled the wings level and finished the choppy flight to Des Moines.

The other half of "Spring Comes to Iowa" was taken while on an exploratory flight over flood waters of the Des Moines River a few days later. In 1948, no flood-control dams had been built on the Des Moines River and it was not unusual for the river to overrun low-lying residential areas of Des Moines. On a gray and overcast March day, the figures in the loaded, horse-drawn wagon blended into the dull flood waters. As I circled to the north, viewing the scene into the hazy light, the silhouette of the family aboard the wagon and the plodding team stood out against the highlighted water. With the wagon directly in the middle of the wide expanse of flood waters, the scene was simple and arresting. Once again, the lighting made the difference.

With the "Spring Comes to Iowa" layout, I had the attention of *Life*'s editors, and they continued during the years following to use photographs originally taken for the *Des Moines Register.* In addition, when I could work around my newspaper responsibilities, I was given direct assignments from *Life.* Editors of other major magazines also offered me assignments, which I accepted when time permitted.

Aerial photographs, images I called "news aerials" because they give the viewer newsworthy information about the subject, won many awards in subsequent years, but the first recognition in a national contest came in 1949 when the *Detroit Times* Annual Feature Award was given my "Spring Seeding" aerial. The photograph was taken while returning late from a flight to the South Dakota–Iowa border. A striking earth scene passed under my wings and I banked the aircraft in a 180-degree turn for a better view. On a gently sloping hillside, black soil was being prepared for seeding. A busy tractor and a dust-raising harrow, strongly backlighted by the sun low in the west, crawled across the dark ground. This was an image worth some time and piloting effort.

After a few sweeping circles, I was able to align the diagonal movement of the plume of dust following the harrow in a position that felt just right. Only one side of a 4 × 5 cut film holder had unexposed film. Just one exposure made, I winged my way back to Des Moines, the light fading rapidly behind the aircraft.

Spring seeding, 1948. *Detroit Times* Feature Award, Kent
State University, 1949.

Aerial photography continued to be an important part of my work. When floods, fires, tornadoes, and blizzards didn't demand our attention, a project we called "Iowa from the Air" kept the plane flying. Starting with the larger cities in Iowa, the *Register* published aerial photographs of all the county seats and many of the smaller picturesque villages in the state. At that time, a view of a city or town from the air offered a glimpse of home most people had not had a chance to see.

In retrospect, the best of my aerial photographs would not have been taken had I faced the problems of talking a pilot into position. The greatest asset I had as a pilot was my 1,300 hours as a primary flight instructor in the Navy, hours and hours of flight near the ground, turns at low level, correcting student mistakes of every kind, and, as a change of pace, aerobatics—loops, Immelmans, inverted spins, and split S's. All of this instilled a deep respect for the limitations of the aircraft and the danger of flying near the ground. At the same time, I learned to be comfortable maneuvering below two or three hundred feet.

Flying with one hand and handling a 4×5 Speed Graphic with the other hand demanded concentration. *U.S. Camera* Editor Tom Maloney commented, "This flying news photographer is busier than a one-armed paper hanger, since he combines work as a pilot, photographer and editor."

The techniques used by aerial photographers in the past did not fill my needs. Conventional, commercial aerial photographers used heavy cameras mounted in the aircraft or held in two hands. Flying high, avoiding turbulence and blurring of the photographer's image due to camera motion, was required because of slow shutter speeds. And, of course, there was always a second person, a pilot, flying the photographer's aircraft.

Also in *U.S. Camera,* in a story entitled "The News Camera A-Wing," I wrote, "Beating photo deadlines by air is part of my job; getting feature pictures which are new and eye-catching is the other part. In the dual capacity of pilot and staff photographer for the *Des Moines Register* and *Tribune* I roam the air over the midwest to bring exclusive news and pictures to our half million subscribers. A 4×5 news camera and a sleek, low-wing plane are the tools of my special trade. Sometimes a reporter is sent with me to the scene of the action, but often I fly alone. This one-man routine is a complete, well-coordinated editorial flight operation. I keep track of only three items: a camera, a plane and myself. I fly the plane and shoot from the left shoulder with a Speed Graphic held in one hand. Knowing the problems of both the aviator and the cameraman is a great advantage in planning and taking better aerial news pictures."

Most aerial photographers preferred a slow, high-wing aircraft; generally, such aircraft have limited window space and a wing strut partially blocking the scene below. My choice was a fast, low-wing plane offering an unobstructed view when the plane was put in a steep bank. By flying low, more dramatic photographs could be made. Further, beating deadlines meant speed was needed.

Because low turns and slow air speed can be dangerous, especially with aerial photography as an added distraction, the answer was to avoid air speeds which could lead to a stall. Low and slow allowed no margin for error; low and fast gave assurance that the plane would not become uncontrollable while my attention was on photography. That, in turn, meant high shutter speeds. The slotted curtain shutter on the Speed Graphic, dependable on a large camera at even a thousandth of a second, was ideal.

On a photo run over the target, the aircraft became a low-flying camera stand responding to the photographer's every thought. Holding the 4×5 Speed Graphic in the right hand and controlling the aircraft with the left hand was a single operation. The aircraft, the camera, the pilot, and the photographer became one.

My pass over a target area was a carefully choreographed *pas de deux*—the photographer with his imagery and the pilot with his survival skills. The target, hidden under the wing as the aircraft closed in, was revealed to my photographic eye as the aircraft rolled into a steep bank. Then the pilot—for the next two or three critical seconds—released the steeply banked aircraft to the photographer. Shutter tripped; photograph taken. Abruptly, the pilot is again in total command. The aircraft quickly rolls into level flight and gains altitude as power is added, elevator trim adjusted, and emergency fields relocated. Each successive pass follows the same process. Overlying this activity is the constant need to avoid rising ground, to monitor wind strength, and to change film holders and dark slides in the camera back. Always, the photograph is paramount: an image with light and shadow, line and form—an eye-arresting, storytelling photograph with a sense of geometry. Persistence is a virtue. Often new corrections for wind drift make each successive low pass more accurate.

As a pilot, I always considered airspeed control the key to survival while photographing at a low altitude. The steep turns required in extreme gustiness complicated control of airspeed. The contour plowing photograph that became part of *Life*'s "Spring Comes to Iowa" in 1948 was taken under turbulent, windy conditions. Faulty air speed control would have been disastrous.

Low and Fast *Gallery II*

The following photographs are all aerials, eye-catching images telling a story and often calling for a second look. When associated with events of the day they can be thought of as news aerials. Others are, in newspaper parlance, feature photographs. It is my hope that all of them have a universality, a timelessness that makes them as appealing today as they were forty years ago.

Most of my storytelling aerials were taken at low altitude. My Speed Graphic was equipped with a normal press photographer's lens, an F:4.5, 135mm Tessar, a slightly wide angle lens by traditional standards. I considered this lens ideal, but to get a good image size, altitudes as low as two hundred feet were often necessary. The first group of the following aerials suggests the advantages of getting close to the subject matter.

Snow plow/snow shovel, 1947.

Madison County tornado, 1947.

Train wreck, 1949.

[NEXT PAGE] Dakota hay lot, 1952. *Life,* with a two-page photographic spread, commented, "In South Dakota snow and cold isolated many a man and beast. [Ranchers] made brief forays out of the house to sled whole stacks of hay, as thickly iced as cupcakes, from fenced-in hay lots out to their hungry herds." Also published in *Amerika,* USIA Russian-language magazine.

Flooded farmstead, 1947. Also included in Steichen's
exhibit *The Exact Instant* at the New York Museum of
Modern Art.

Island farmstead, 1949. *Life*'s caption: "When the West Nishnabotna River approached the 600-acre farm of Leroy Sudger, the family fled. But the farmyard, wisely built on the highest land, stayed dry, saving 13 head of cattle and 100 chickens."

Damming the Missouri at Fort Randall, South Dakota, 1951. *U.S. Camera Annual 1954,* stated, "Almost a bas-relief, it is informative graphically as well as interesting photographically." This photograph was also reproduced, full page, in *Amerika.*

Man faces raging river, 1953. This photograph was taken
just before the torrent swept away man and house. On the
next pass over the site, both were gone.

Big Ditch, 1950. Top news picture of the year (tied with
Life photographer Mark Kauffman) in 1951 Great Pictures
competition, awarded by the University of Missouri
School of Journalism and the *Encyclopaedia Britannica*
judges.

Pelican flight, Nishnabotna River, 1955.

Wintertime offers a special opportunity for simple, uncomplicated aerial images. The mantle of snow obliterates distracting detail, and objects stand out in stark relief against the all-encompassing backdrop of white.

Currier and Ives, 1947. A horse drawn bobsled. Part of the *U.S. Camera 1954* portfolio. Editor Tom Maloney: "The design of an artist's work, the reality of winter on the farm, the sentimentality of a Christmas card combine to bring the nostalgia of a children's holiday in the country." Also, *Photography Annual 1954*.

Steam train, 1948.

Horses/winterscape, 1952. Tom Maloney, editor of *U.S.
Camera Annual 1954* stated, "The famous aerial technique
of Don Ultang has been used here to depict a typical Iowa
winter scene. It is his ability to compose his pictures
artistically while photographing from the air which makes
this work so outstanding. He has caught all the cold
loneliness and isolation which match the beauty of the
spacious midwestern plains in the winter." Also,
Photography Annual 1954.

Top of the world, 1951.

Dakota winter, 1951.

Winter rescue, 1951.

Old world church, 1952.

Church at Read, 1951. >

Country school, 1954.

Frozen Mississippi, 1951. >

Winner, South Dakota, 1954.

Bomber crash, Lone Tree, 1955. >

Eventide, 1952.

Thunderstorms, 1947.

Illinois farm fire, 1956.

In a B-29 over Omaha, 1953.

Rainmaker, 1947.

The Navy a-wing, 1952. For a moment the *Register*'s
Beechcraft is flight leader of a Navy formation including a
TBM torpedo bomber and an F8F fighter.

Mid-air refueling, 1954. A Strategic Air Command B-47
refuels from an Air Force tanker.

The strong appeal of form *(geometry,* as stated by Cartier-Bresson) is often evident from the air. The sense of abstract composition, an image wherein line and mass are more important than specific subject matter, dominates the view. Some examples follow.

Plowing abstractionist, 1949. Graflex Corporation, makers of the Speed Graphic and allied cameras, published this photograph as the frontispiece in its last edition of the *Graphic Graflex Photography Manual,* the guide for decades of photographers.

Mississippi River, snow and ice, 1950.

The burning land, 1955. (ABOVE) March winds blow away
top soil. (BELOW) Monolith, 1955. Earth work at South
Dakota dam site.

Corn shocks, 1956.

Last threshing days, 1951.

Windrows, 1951.

Fingers of flood, 1952. *Life*'s comment: "Flooding
Missouri caught on the march. Here, in this picture, a
flood is shown actually on the march. It was taken by *Des
Moines Register* photographer Don Ultang, five miles
south of Plum Creek dike which had crumbled under the
weight of the Missouri River." Also, *U.S. Camera Annual
1953*.

Ultang in Swift aircraft (*Good News VIII*).

Mollenhoff in same aircraft (*Good News VIII*).

First Register and Tribune Beechcraft Bonanza *(Good News IX)* in flight.

Hometown paper for the whole state of Iowa...

why?

because of its air photos?

Well, that's part of the reason The Register and Tribune is flying high in Iowa. Back in 1928, "Good News I" became an exciting addition to its news-gathering facilities. Today, when news is made ...whether it's a political meteor flashing to prominence or a brilliant halfback dashing to a winning score... the sleek, swift "Good News XI" rushes stories and pictures to the newsroom in Des Moines. It travels more than 60,000 miles a year to help The Register and Tribune publish the kind of papers that have won perhaps the most unusual circulation in America. Its papers are read by 70% of the whole state of Iowa!

DES MOINES REGISTER AND TRIBUNE

350,000 COMBINED DAILY · 500,000 SUNDAY

Gardner Cowles, President

Pulitzer Prize winner and flying photographer Don Ultang and "Good News XI" are a familiar sight all over Iowa.

A *New Yorker* ad, 1958.

3

Journalism and the Unobtrusive Camera

Metropolitan newspapers in 1940, the year I joined the nine-man news photography staff of the *Register* and *Tribune,* had little concern for esoteric photojournalistic efforts; hard news pictures and photographs to supplement feature stories filled the assignment sheets. A 4 × 5 Speed Graphic with a flash bulb the size of a regular light bulb was standard; I inherited a smaller, less desirable 3¼ × 4¼ Speed Graphic. Occasionally, the opportunity to produce a well-composed scene arose, but persistence and a sense of newsworthiness counted for more than subtleties of lighting, composition, or the role of the unobtrusive camera.

A good news photograph was in sharp focus, exhibited no waste space and was newsworthy. An excellent art department, skilled in airbrush techniques, salvaged many flash photographs by removing extraneous material or applying a lighter tone to an otherwise completely black background.

News photographers regularly chased ambulances to hospital emergency rooms where accident victims were photographed while awaiting treatment. The pressure of deadlines and the use of a camera the size of a football didn't prevent the editors from asking for variety on the news pages. Photographers tried different poses, different props and tricks to produce "something different."

This method of operation, while rewarding persistence and directness rather than insightfulness and unobtrusiveness, produced photographs of importance when the event itself was significant. Even with its limitations, both physical and philosophical, the Speed Graphic was a dependable, no-nonsense workhorse capturing newsworthy images when placed in the hands of a knowledgeable news photographer, and for a number of years it continued to be the news photographers' camera.

Just prior to the war, girls' basketball was in the early stages of developing dedicated fans over all of Iowa; a state tournament for girls held in Des Moines annually was becoming a frenzied event. Firing a monstrous, oversized flashbulb synchronized with the Speed Graphic's large focal plane shutter (a black, cloth curtain with a number of horizontal slots), I was in the right place to record a photographic first at an Iowa state girls' basketball tourney by capturing – at the moment the game ended – the losers, not the winners. The photograph I took of the losers sobbing as they streamed off the court was sent to *Life,* unknown to me and over my signature, by the *Register's* promotion department with the accompanying letter: "The girls from Ottosen, Iowa High School team were mightily disappointed when after leading the Numa, Iowa girls through most of their quarter-final game in the state basketball tournament, they lost 41–35. When the final gun sounded the girls broke into tears and walked off the floor downcast." Published in the "Picture to the Editors" section of *Life* at the back of the magazine, it was a small photo, about five by six inches – not artistic, but it had human interest. In any event, being published in *Life* was the ultimate for any newspaper photographer known to me, and I was grateful.

During this period, two major photographic assignments, separated by a period of five years and, again, both far removed from the insightful, unobtrusive approach to photojournalism, warrant comment. One, the coverage of Winston Churchill's historic 1946 Iron Curtain speech in Fulton, Missouri, was nearly a disaster. The other, a 1951 sports assignment covering a college football game in Stillwater, Oklahoma, won a Pulitzer Prize.

The Churchill assignment, a competitive, tumultuous gathering of news photographers forced to work on a catch-as-catch-can basis, resembled the coverage of a major track event more than a world class speech. The football game in Oklahoma produced a Pulitzer Prize, a great honor, but a Pulitzer Prize in Spot News Photography has more to do with the photographer's quick reactions in an emergency than with the storytelling abilities of the photographer. Any photograph winning the Spot News category attests to the photographer's good fortune – being at the site of a single newsworthy event of major proportions. Killings, fires, mob scenes, war destruction, vehicle smash-ups, and drownings dominate Spot News winners. Historically, only spot news photographs were allowed in the annual competition. In 1968, a second category called Feature Photography was added, basing that award on a group of photographs developing a single theme.

The slugging of Johnny Bright on a football field in north-central Oklahoma, the Spot News winner in 1952, does not represent the subtle images of the photojournalism of W. Eugene Smith or Alfred Eisenstaedt. It does suggest the value of being in the right place at the right time. More significantly, it brought the recognition of racial prejudice into the consciousness of sport fans across the country.

Five years before the Johnny Bright incident a significant turning point in the history of international relationships took place in mid-America (early 1946). To be a part of such an event is one of the values of being a journalist and is a very satisfying experience, and the *Register* assigned the coverage to me.

Winston Churchill, speaking in the chapel at Westminster College in the small town of Fulton, Missouri, told the world that the USSR was dropping an iron curtain between western and eastern Europe. This Iron Curtain speech marked the start of the Cold War. President Harry S. Truman, in Fulton to welcome Churchill to Missouri and introduce him to those gathered in the chapel, had invited England's war-time prime minister to this little-known town in Truman's home state. Although news coverage was the domain of black and white photography, *Register* editors wanted staff color photographs for the Sunday Rotogravure section. George Mills, reporter for the *Register,* and Cliff Millen, reporter for the *Tribune,* drove with me from Des Moines to Fulton into the late hours of the evening in my well-traveled 1934 Plymouth.

The next day all the photographers, those in the Washington, D.C. press corps as well as representatives from all the larger midwestern cities, heard the bad news. The usual vantage point below the speaker's platform was out-of-bounds. All my planning, all my thoughts of various juxtapositions of Churchill and Truman and the expectation of a selection of activities and close-up facial expressions were to no avail. The twenty or twenty-five photographers were to be kept at the rear of Westminster's large chapel, a distance of eighty to one hundred feet to the dais. On a pre-arranged signal we would be allowed to move forward to a position about twenty-five feet from Churchill, Truman, and the other dignitaries.

This photo opportunity would be brief—two or three moments into the forward position—possibly repeated a second time. In the dimly lighted, cavernous chapel there would be no opportunity to refocus our large press cameras. Probably I would be forced to take my photographs at an undetermined distance. As it turned out, the signal to go forward released such a rush of desperate photographers that finding the pre-arranged position was impossible. With no time to refocus the camera, an educated guess had to be right. My new position wasn't ideal, but we were ordered almost immediately to return to the rear of the auditorium. Handling flash bulbs and the press camera film holders was a well-developed skill, but I only had time for two exposures.

The far reaches of the auditorium were dark and the color film then in use was not very light sensitive. Available light exposure, using whatever natural and artificial light the building offered, was impossible. Maximum lens openings were modest on press cameras, and the flash bulbs on which we relied were normally not used beyond fifteen feet. Working under these conditions was a challenge to all the photographers there. We had one more rush forward and an immediate order to retreat. The opportunity to photograph Churchill's Fulton, Missouri, speech was over as quickly as it had started. The marginal conditions were troublesome, but I felt I had something of value in my film holders.

After the formal speech Churchill and Truman retired to the college president's quarters. Newspaper and magazine people patrolled the lawn waiting for any further developments. Suddenly, Churchill and Truman, in dark business suits, were out on the lawn standing together watching as we scrambled for good shooting positions. This provided us with backup photographs. The brilliant red of the robes worn in the chapel setting gave the *Register* editors the color hoped for and none of these secondary photographs were used.

This close look on the lawn made the physical contrast between Churchill and Truman striking. The Briton of massive head and bulldog countenance was nonetheless cheerful as he lighted a cigar. Truman, standing ramrod erect as opposed to Churchill's hunched over position, was in charge. He ordered the photographers not to take pictures while Churchill was lighting his cigar. As the match flared I saw this as a golden opportunity for a photograph that was different and interesting—and typically Churchillian. Ironically, the photograph was neither revealing nor interesting and was not used.

Churchill at Fulton, Missouri, 1946.

The disorderly and brief photo opportunities while Churchill was delivering his Iron Curtain speech produced two color transparencies to the liking of our Rotogravure editor. Bright colors always help and Churchill's scarlet robes created an attention-getting layout. Extra care in the printing process produced pictures in the Sunday *Register* which overcame the less-than-ideal transparencies.

Five years later, ideal flying weather and an assignment in Oklahoma allowed two *Register* photographers to win a Pulitzer Prize for coverage of a football game surrounded by a controversy great enough to cause the withdrawal of Drake University from the Missouri Valley Conference.

Today, college football has been made an overwhelming commercial and entertainment force through the medium of television, but America's fascination with the game began years before the 1951 football assignment. It grew as part of the awakening of big time sports between World War I and the great Depression of the thirties. Many newspapers responded by enlarging their sports departments.

As sports interest grew, great numbers of football fans learned to love the game. Names such as Red Grange, the galloping ghost of Illinois, Knute Rockne and his Four Horsemen at Notre Dame, and the Seven Blocks of Granite at Fordham made headlines each Saturday. Babe Ruth in baseball, Barney Oldfield in auto racing, Bobby Jones in golf, Jack Dempsey and Gene Tunney in boxing, and Bill Tilden and Helen Wills in tennis became famous. They were idolized. Radio had its part in this growing national sports consciousness, but the printed page with photographs and stories fed the interest of sports lovers. Only newspapers could show the countless numbers of fans the images and weekly exploits of famous football personalities.

The American devotion to football continued to grow. After World War II, with television yet to make its impact on the sports scene, the *Des Moines Register* responded to the intense interest in college football. Flying a company-owned airplane to meet deadlines and offering its readers staff-produced, diagramed action photographs the newspaper became nationally recognized for its excellent football coverage. Before the days of television the diagramed football photograph visually dramatized football action as newspaper sports sections were read in America's homes. The diagramed photo was the big-screen sports visual of the forties and fifties.

The Sunday Register named its Big Peach sports section for the color of the newsprint. Sports coverage helped build the circulation to more than 500,000 in the decade of the fifties and probably reached three times as many readers.

Every Saturday during the football season photographic crews were flown to the two or three most important games in the Midwest for exclusive staff coverage. Big Ten and Big Eight games were our principal targets, and Notre Dame games were often on our schedule. Our goal in all cases was to photograph dramatic action in the early stages of a game, rush to our readied plane, and fly to Des Moines to meet the Sunday first edition deadline. I piloted our company plane—a single-engine Beechcraft Bonanza—on the longest flight each Saturday and chartered aircraft for the other crews.

For the major game of the day, we sent two cameramen, one with a Bell and Howell Eyemo movie camera altered to take still photographs at four frames per second (a rarity forty years ago) and one with a modified 4×5 camera equipped with a long lens capable of producing large images from a great distance. The lens, a full 20 inches long because quality telephoto lenses were not available for 4×5 cameras, was used with a Speed Graphic back and a slotted-curtain shutter and was housed in a custom-designed metal tube more than two feet in length.

Upon arrival at a stadium we did what television crews do today. We found a location in the upper reaches of the press box and set up tripods and cameras so as to give us the best vantage point for the game action. As television demands were yet to come we were able to find prime viewing space. Some universities such as Ohio State and Notre Dame gave us space adjacent to the sportswriters, thus protecting us from the rain and snow. Northwestern University had limited space forcing us to work on an open roof. The climb up the flat ladder on the side of the wooden press box with our heavy equipment was always a challenge. A day with sleet and a strong northwest wind made the problem even more difficult.

The *Register* diagramed all football photographs in the Sunday Big Peach section. The reader was shown either a sequence of five to eight small photographs or large single photographs. The diagramed photographs gave the reader all vital information: the ball carrier, his course as he ran, blocking assignments, and defensive action. A skilled staff of graphic artists made the diagramed photos possible. The diagraming—

with the addition of written explanations from the sports identifier who traveled with the photo crew—gave the reader a clear understanding of the dramatic views of the game: instant replay on the newspaper page.

A major variable in the *Register's* football coverage each Saturday was the weather. In the Midwest, as fall blends into early winter, bad flying weather can arrive in many forms: low ceilings and poor visibility, heavy fog, snow, sleet and, most deadly, freezing rain; strong headwinds could become a major problem in meeting deadlines. On some days of marginal weather, we made flights when few other single-engine aircraft were in the air.

Fortunately the universities farthest from Des Moines were in the eastern time zone. In the Big Ten, Ohio State at Columbus and Michigan at Ann Arbor were the greatest challenges and only possible because of the hour gained when flying west. Because of prevailing winds in the northern hemisphere, a headwind was almost always encountered. Occasionally, extremely treacherous weather forced flights already airborne to find safety on the ground.

Return flights often meant many hours in the air with the range and cruising speed of the aircraft stretched to the limit. The coverage of the University of Iowa season opener at Pittsburgh in 1957 was a singular effort in that regard. Sports fans in Iowa that fall were excited about a new season for a promising University of Iowa football team. Exclusive coverage by the *Register's* staff photographers was in keeping with the reputation of the Big Peach sports section. On the return flight, time in the air was critical. With extra fuel tanks filled, we left the rough country-side of Pennsylvania, flying steadily westward past Cleveland and Toledo into the middle of Indiana. The headwinds at our cruising altitude of 8,500 feet were mild until we sighted the gray smudge of South Chicago at the southern tip of Lake Michigan. As we flew toward the Mississippi River and homebase, the sun lowered toward the western horizon and headwinds steadily increased. Our first-edition deadline was missed by a few minutes that Saturday, but other editions brought our Iowa-Pittsburgh coverage to more than 90 percent of our Sunday readers.

Never, with all our dedication and experience, did any of us give a thought to a Pulitzer Prize in news photography. Many capable photojournalists produce dramatic images for their newspapers each day, but the chance of any photograph winning such a prize is always small. The odds of a sports photograph winning a Pulitzer Prize is even smaller.

There is, of course, more than one way to win this prize: a wartime winner was Joe Rosenthal, who took the famous photograph of planting the American flag on Iwo Jima. Amateur Arnold Hardy, a student at Georgia Tech, won in 1947 with a photograph of a woman's body hurtling to destruction from the upper floors of a burning Atlanta hotel, the Winecoff. Another amateur, Virginia Schau, won the 1954 Pulitzer Prize using the family snapshot camera, a Kodak Brownie, when she photographed a truck driver in the cab of his truck hanging precariously over a California ravine, forty feet deep. In 1989, Ron Olshwager, a Missouri furniture company executive, took a photograph of a firefighter trying to resuscitate a little girl, and Olshwager became the third amateur to win a Pulitzer Prize.

John Robinson and I were co-winners in 1952 for a series of sports photographs taken on a sunny Saturday in October at a football game in Stillwater, Oklahoma. The game was characterized in the *New York Times* (November 13, 1985) as "one of the ugliest racial incidents in college sports history," and our presence there was an unlikely happening for many reasons. First of all, we were covering a game in a location that had never been on our flight schedule. Although Drake University games at home were given excellent photographic coverage, we did not regularly fly a crew to games away from Drake's home field. Primarily, however, the prize would be won because Drake University, meeting an all-white team, brought a nationally lauded black football player to Stillwater. The black player would be slugged into unconsciousness four times in seven minutes. The blows were never whistled by the officials, and sports writers from the vantage point of the press box were not certain at that time how it had happened.

The reality of racial bias on the college playing field was forced into the American consciousness when these photographs were published. These telling images were printed in major newspapers in the nation. *Life* magazine displayed them in a page-and-a-half layout. Drake University left the Missouri Valley Conference in protest. The photographs prompted a new rule calling for automatic disqualification for a player caught striking an opponent with "forearm, elbow or locked hand."

On that October day in 1951 Johnny Bright, born in Fort Wayne, Indiana, became "a black hero in a white man's world" in the opinion of Maury White, who was in the Lewis Field press box for the *Register* in Stillwater that day. When Bright died suddenly 32 years later, a reporter at the *Register* asked me for a comment. Recalling that day and the incriminating photographs, my comment was, "the incident pointed out a social problem that hadn't been recognized in the sports world; suddenly America found out a black man could be knocked around deliberately. It brought a consciousness to the collegiate sports world that had not been there before." Fans in every state were given direct, positive evidence of racial bias in college football.

Winner of their first five games, the Drake Bulldogs traveled to play the Aggies of Oklahoma A&M (now Oklahoma State University). With rumors circulating that this talented black athlete was going to be stopped by the Aggies one way or another, Bright stayed with a black minister several miles from the rest of the Drake team. At that time, he had gained more yards than any man in collegiate history. In the previous two years, Bright had led the nation in total offense, and in the current year he was continuing as number one in the country. The Bulldog halfback excelled at running and passing and made Drake's offense work. The combination of Bright's national reputation and rumors regarding his possible reception by the Aggies made this an important game to cover. There was a problem of a delayed arrival in Des Moines if we had strong northerly headwinds on our return flight. We concluded it was worth the risk. As it turned out, an unusual weather pattern developed during the game day, and brisk southwesterly winds gave us an extremely fast journey home.

On that warm, breezy Saturday, with more than 12,000 Aggies football fans starting to crowd into the stadium, John Robinson and I set up our tripods and cameras in the press box. Our most experienced photo identifier, Bob Spiegel, later to become editor of the *Mason City Globe-Gazette* and eventually editor of the *Wisconsin State Journal,* was a third pair of eyes in our photo crew at Stillwater. Robinson had a Bell and Howell Eyemo camera designed to capture sequence photographs of the ball carrier in action. I had our large, single-exposure camera, which produced an overall image of the activity on the field. An enlargement could be diagramed to show a general view of a single, critical moment during any one play. Making the exposure at the right moment was a matter of experience and instinct. Once an exposure had been made, it was impossible to take a second photograph during the same play.

Bright was on the field for seven minutes only and for very few plays. Repeatedly knocked senseless, the halfback returned each time, only to lie sprawling on the ground again and again. Bright was neither the ball carrier nor the passer the first three times he was slugged. On three nearly identical plays, starting with the first play of the game when Drake made five yards, Bright, well away from the play action, somehow took blows that in each case left him senseless on the grass. Because Robinson and I were tracking the ball carrier as well as trying to keep an eye on Bright, we were unclear how Bright had been knocked unconscious. We both thought our film would tell the story, but we were far from certain.

Following the first slugging, helpers went out on the field, clustering around their downed team leader. After a few moments, Bright was on his feet, still dazed. He stayed in the game. On second down, with five yards to go, Bright lined up at tailback in the single wing formation, stumbling briefly as he looked downfield for a receiver. Bending backward awkwardly, Bright lofted a pass as high as a punt and as long. Bright was still groggy as a Drake receiver raced under the ball near the goal line and ran into the end zone. A 61-yard pass play!

The Aggies failed to make a first down but scored a touchdown after intercepting a wobbly Bright pass. With Drake leading 7–6, and in possession of the ball on its 13-yard line, the Bulldog's star halfback again handed off on a running play over left tackle. A two yard gain—Bright, again, was lying prone and unconscious.

Few had watched Bright after each hand off. Robinson and I continued in the effort to watch both the ball carrier and Bright, but a number of yards separated them each time a play was finished. Spiegel, our identifier, thought the Aggies' left tackle had bumped into Bright, but overt slugging in the open seemed unbelievable. Not until the film was processed in the *Register* photographic lab were we certain of the whole story. After each hand-off, Bright stood, arms relaxed at his side, watching the play develop as the ball carrier probed left tackle. From Bright's blind side, his right, the Aggies' defensive left tackle, untouched by anyone, bore down on the black player—smashing his weight and forearm into the halfback's jaw.

The large single photographs showed clearly the impact as the Aggies' fist and forearm met a waiting face. Robinson, with the sequence camera, had a series of frames on his film showing, at the top and right of each frame, the Aggie tackle leaving the line of scrimmage and working his way without hinderance to reach an unsuspecting Bright. The cam-

Des Moines Sunday Register *Sports*

DES MOINES, IOWA, SUNDAY, OCTOBER 21, 1951.

IOWA FAILS, 21-0; IOWA STATE WINS

(Bert McGrane's Story on Page 3.)   (Brad Wilson's Story on Page 5.)

Bright's Jaw Broken, Drake Streak Ends, 27-14

JOHNNY HURT ON FIRST PLAY, THEN HURLS SCORING PASS (STORY: PAGE 8)

EVER SEE A JAW BROKEN?—On the first scrimmage play of the Drake-Oklahoma Aggie game Saturday at Stillwater, Okla., Drake's John Bright is shown as he hands the ball to a teammate, then moves out of the action. As he watches his teammate charge toward the line, two Aggie defenders close in on him. One turns off toward the Bulldog with the ball, but Wilbanks Smith of the Aggies has only eyes for Bright. Smith cocks his right fist (Picture No. 5 above), then drives it into Bright's jaw (No. 6). Picture No. 7 (the top part of the photo below) shows the overall scene. Note every player, except Smith, is watching the ball carrier. Bright was knocked down on the play. (X-rays later showed Bright's jaw was broken). Even this didn't stop Bright. A moment later he threw a 61-yard touchdown pass. But the bottom part of the picture below shows what happened to Bright a few minutes later. Again Wilbanks Smith goes for Bright, who is out of the play—about eight yards behind the Drake ball carrier. Other Aggies converge on the Bulldog runner. Not Smith. Bright's head goes back like a fighter being knocked out. And this was the end of John Bright—probably for the season. He was half carried, half led off the field (Picture on Page 5).

JOHN BRIGHT'S FIRST PLAY...

...AND HERE'S THE FINISHER

Bright on the ground, unconscious. Hitherto unpublished, this is the result of the third slugging of Johnny Bright. He only lasted ten plays, and Drake lost 14–27.

< The Johnny Bright slugging, 1951. Awarded the 1952 Pulitzer Prize for news photography to John Robinson and Don Ultang. Also, *U.S. Camera Annual 1953*. And *Life*.

eras, capturing evidence regarding which no witness at the game could be certain, showed both the intent and the viciousness of the attacks. Bright was revived the second time and stayed in the game a few more plays — long enough to be slugged senseless the third and fourth time.

The *Register* sports editor White, a fine Drake tailback in his own right years earlier, reported in his game story: "Bright, again minus the ball, collided violently with 200-pound senior left tackle Wilbanks Smith. Johnny was down again. [For the third time Drake trainer Mankowski was back on the field.] Bright eventually got up rubbing his jaw tenderly. The next play was it. The versatile guy who has survived for almost three years of concentrated attention went gallantly plugging around right end."

A great pile up of players overwhelmed Bright on his last play. As before, the trainer and a reserve guard half-led and half-carried the nation's leading offensive back to the Drake bench. No penalties had been called. He never entered the game again. Later X-rays determined that his jaw was broken, probably from the first blow.

Drake lost that game, 14–27. A reinjury to Bright's jaw reoccurred two weeks later, causing his absence in the last game of the season.

The Bulldogs' great halfback went on to a fine record as a Canadian football player even though he was the number-one draft choice of the Philadelphia Eagles. After his football career ended, he became a highly respected high school principal in Canada. He died in 1983. The following year he was inducted posthumously into the National Collegiate Hall of Fame. On his death the *Edmonton Journal* said, in part: "A black man, he battled racism with his deeds while lesser men cowered in the face of injustice. He brought the example of his inner strength among our young men and women as a teacher and a leader. His students wept at his loss. It was fitting."

Even in the days when the Speed Graphic was considered *de rigueur* there were occasional opportunities to produce images that were not only informative but with a sense of significance beyond the immediate. Between the rush to cover spot news stories (fires, automobile accidents or a manslaughter suspect held at the county jail), there were times when wonderful moments materialized. An old coal tipple at the edge of Centerville, a small county seat in southern Iowa, combined a sense of an era out of the distant past, compelling lines, and the texture of old timbers. It demanded to be photographed for its stark beauty. Winter street scenes in Des Moines recalled the photography of Alfred Stieglitz. Zoot suits and bobby sox in a night club on Center Street, just west of Keosauqua Way in Des Moines, were riveting to the eye. And the girls' basketball games, the center of wintertime pride and social activity in many Iowa small towns, provided action photographs with balance and a sense of proportion. Despite the bulky Speed Graphic, a news photographer, given the desire, could produce images with lasting eye-appeal and a feeling of universality.

In the offing, however, were changes in photojournalism and in photography as an art form. Smaller cameras and faster emulsions would give unfettered movement to the photographer; this freedom, hopefully coupled with insight and perception, would change the way we looked at ourselves and our neighbors.

Photographers for *Life* and other major publications showed the world what could be done with 35mm cameras and a new unobtrusive approach to authenticity. Certainly the realization that journalistic photography could be sensitive, intimate, and artistic was becoming recognized, thus bringing to the printed page a new view of the twentieth century. In his strongest statement regarding the new approach, Henri Cartier-Bresson espoused "the decisive moment" principle as the truest form of practicing photojournalism.

The flexibility and adaptability of the 35mm camera was important, but this new view indicated that the thinking process of photographers had changed as well. The many general-interest national magazines then being published demanded a more natural, realistic approach. In addition to *Life,* the editors of *Look, American Magazine, Collier's, Woman's Home Companion, Holiday, Pageant,* and *Fortune* used photographers who understood picture-story techniques, photographers who could produce compassionate, candid, and authentic images. Newspapers, however, were reluctant to change from the Speed Graphic approach for a number of reasons. The cost of the change was an important factor, but most newspaper editors were not yet demanding that their photographers match the insightfulness and naturalness that characterized the work of leading magazine photographers of the time.

By contrast, photojournalists such as Marc Riboud, a founding member with Cartier-Bresson of the famous Magnum Photo Group, believed in "lasting moments," enduring images offering the viewer material for reflection. These were images calling for a thoughtful second response, a contemplative consideration holding the viewer beyond the initial impact. These were images – visual experiences – to be savored for their power of suggestion. *Life's* Alfred Eisenstaedt, frequently described as "the father of photojournalism," stated the photojournalist's job is "to find and catch the storytelling moment." Eisenstaedt, Cartier-Bresson, and contemporaries such as W. Eugene Smith would influence a generation of photographers who believed photojournalism and artistry were natural partners.

Julia Scully, editor of *Modern Photography* and long-time observer of photographic trends, in the October 1985 issue stated, "In retrospect the decade of the fifties was a uniquely dramatic time in photography, a time that witnessed the apex of photojournalism."

Historically, news photographers started as apprentices in the engraving department or as darkroom assistants. Newspapers, slow to recognize the changing emphasis in the world of photojournalism, continued to view their photographers as technicians. Having learned to produce sharp images with a Speed Graphic was considered sufficient, even if the resulting images offered little insight into the subject being photographed. But in the middle fifties, a few young newspaper photographers, responding to the example of leading magazine photographers, broke new ground for their newspaper readers. Some would eventually leave their newspapers for magazine work. From the *Milwaukee Journal* Howard Sochurek moved to *Life* magazine and Thomas Abercrombie, the newspaper photographer of the year award-winner in 1954, became a valuable addition to the staff of the *National Geographic.* The *Denver Post* saw Carl Iwasaki become a photographer for *Life*, and the *Post's* Dean Conger started traveling the world for *National Geographic.* Trained as journalists, these photographers brought to their work a broad understanding of their society and a feeling for the people they photographed.

The *National Geographic* – long the stronghold of posed, picture-postcard presentations – in the late forties and fifties began "telling stories with pictures," in the words of Conger. And Robert Gilka, appointed *National Geographic's* director of photography in 1963, was in an excellent position to see the results of changes originating in the late forties and early fifties. "In the early days *Geographic* photographers came up through the lab – they were technicians who later got into photographic reportage. The new people were trained as photojournalists." Gilka believes the main difference between the older and newer group of photographers was the way they approached picture taking. "The traditional darkroom-trained photographer wanted a clear, sharp, exposed picture — a brilliant print from the negative. The photojournalists tended to be more concerned with what's going on in the photograph. They gained reputations as image-makers."

Sometime early in this post-war period I concluded that a sense of proportion (Cartier-Bresson's *geometry)* and a greater authenticity could both properly be goals of daily newspaper photographers. In a 1954 article in *The Quill,* a monthly magazine devoted to journalism, I commented on such forces at work at the newspaper level. Raising a challenge, I stated "many news photographers are being constantly beaten on feature and picture story assignments by photojournalists with a greater understanding and a more acute response to the intangibles involved.

"The news man must change his thinking about the 'time value' of his pictures. A photograph that is great is one which will be worth looking at ten or twenty years from now — not just until the next edition. This means the news photographer must not only recognize news worthy subject matter. He must also work with those subtle factors which give lasting value to a photograph long after the original timelessness has vanished. To do this he must borrow from the understanding and techniques of the photo interpreter, the Cartier-Bressons, the Eisenstaedts, and Steichens. These men might have been news photographers, but they are more than that. They are photojournalists in the largest sense.

"This means the news photographer must bring greater understanding to his subject matter. He must weave into his work the highly important elements of lighting and composition to give his photographs greater authenticity and storytelling impact.

"The news photographer is in the most advantageous position to turn out today's greatest photographs. There is no more fertile field for the person who wants to deal directly with reality and at the same time apply whatever degree of artistry he (or she) can bring to bear on the situation. This artistry is more than adequate consideration of lighting and composition, although both factors are vital. It is a feeling for the intangibles which tells the photographer what the proper elements are in any given situation. Composition is often less mechanical than many photographers realize. Perhaps the term 'arrangement' is a good substitute. However, Frank Lloyd Wright's definition means even more. He calls it a 'sense of proportion.' A 'sense of proportion' takes into consideration much more than arbitrary rules of composition. The latter make a good starting point, but it is only by much thought and understanding that we can finally take all the elements of a changing situation and combine subject matter, lighting and basic composition into an image having a sense of proportion."

A few of us on the staff of the *Register* and *Tribune* responded to these new challenges and started covering assignments with 35mm cameras, striving for photographs with impact and storytelling appeal. We learned to produce picture stories with a sense of authenticity and to capture individual photographs that were arresting, revealing, and informative—and contained a sense of proportion. Photographs of such quality that they would be considered first class images in any period, present or future, became my personal goal. That it might be history in the making did not occur to me.

Other than aerial photographs, my most significant work after 1950 was produced with a 35mm rangefinder Leica. Adaptation to 35mm cameras was made by others on the newspaper staff, leading to a complete swing to 35mm over the next ten years. This was an exciting and challenging period, as the use of the 35mm camera and the unobtrusive, authentic approach to photographic coverage opened before me. The following events give insight into my effort to record my feeling for the subject matter and my sense of the moment. Here I struggled to capture the sense of being on the scene—the real essence of each story—on film.

A harsh blizzard swept over eastern Nebraska and western Iowa in late November, 1952. The weather had deteriorated the day before Thanksgiving, but no meteorologist had predicted a uniquely punishing early winter storm. Believing we would be able to make a late-night return, a reporter and I had driven to Omaha for a Sunday feature story. By late Wednesday afternoon, U.S. Highway 6 (later paralleled by Interstate 80) east to Des Moines was reported blocked. We decided to stay overnight in Omaha and checked into a downtown hotel. At midnight the wind, howling and gusting, was driving snow through the streets and stopping automobile traffic.

A day or two before the Omaha trip, *Life* magazine had put in my hands a new lens for my Leica, a Japanese lens. At that time, Japan was beginning to make a worldwide impression as a producer of superior cameras and lenses. *Life* had tested a number of lenses and eventually purchased some for use by its staff photographers. In addition, some photographers in whom the magazine had a special interest were given the opportunity to buy these lenses. In any event, the Leica and the lens were both new to me. A press camera was still the basic tool for *Register* staff photographers.

My ideas regarding the use of a 35mm camera for newspaper work had started to form, but none had been put to use. A blizzard at midnight was an appealing subject for a camera with a fast Nikkor lens (F:1.4). Lightweight and mobile, this combination might open new vistas, and experimentation was appealing.

Outside, the whipping wind and stinging snow made movement difficult. Night shadows were deep; street lights and signs glowed strangely. Through the veil of snow two men huddled against a building half a block away. Under these conditions, proper exposure was impossible to determine. With the camera at the slowest shutter speed appropriate to a hand-held camera ($\frac{1}{15}$th of a second) and the lens at maximum aperture I made an exposure of the empty street, strange lights, parked cars, and wind-driven snow.

The powerful forces at work made this a wonderful scene. The exposure had just been made when one of the two men started dashing across the street about fifty yards away. Startled into action, I hastily turned the film transport knob, put the camera to my eye, and waited a count or two until the wraith-like figure was in the open, set apart by the glowing lights. It was an exciting moment, and it might be an exciting photograph. Back in Des Moines, the film was given careful treatment and my best skills were put into the enlargement.

The snow storm was on the negative. The sense of the raging wind, the driving snow, and a lone figure running through the winter night made a strong image. A feeling of holding the moment for all to see was very real. In addition to the *Register, Life* gave the photograph a full page. In connection with their publishing a portfolio of my work, the editors of *U.S. Camera Annual 1954* also used this picture as the lead photograph in their advertising campaign. As a photographer who believes that photojournalism should, whenever possible, combine reality with whatever touch of artistry can be applied, I believe this may be my finest single photograph.

Blizzard at midnight, 1952. "Spectral pedestrian scampers across a deserted street swept by flurries of snow in downtown Omaha at the height of the big storm," wrote *Life*. Editors of *U.S. Camera Annual*, in using this image as a lead photograph, commented, "One of Don Ultang's greatest attributes is his ability to make one picture representative of all similar situations. The elements of the stormy winter night are so deftly combined that it becomes all blizzards, everywhere." Also, *Photography Annual 1954*.

There were other situations in which the split-second capabilities of 35mm were used to advantage.

Sitting Bull, the powerful Sioux chieftain, was buried at Fort Yates, North Dakota, after dying under questionable conditions while in the custody of the U.S. Army. On a snowy night in March, 1953, Sioux Indians from South Dakota, descendants of Sitting Bull, exhumed the bones of Sitting Bull and took them back to Mobridge, South Dakota. This area of the Dakotas had been Sitting Bull's homeland. His people, with the help of white sympathizers, wanted to bring his remains back to his own land.

The news services carried the story, which prompted the *Register* news editor to send reporter Knox Craig with me on Friday to Mobridge for a Sunday story. We planned an overnight in Mobridge, but the return on a Saturday had to meet the usual first edition deadline. Craig was able to get background material from non-Indian attorneys and sympathizers in Mobridge, but at the end of our first day we had seen only one Sioux connected with the reburial activity.

Whatever Craig's need to talk directly to a member of Sitting Bull's family, my problem was greater. A photograph without the descendants of the famous chief was worthless. On Saturday morning, not many hours before our Des Moines deadline, we finally arranged to meet members of the tribal council in an effort to bring the principals together for a photograph. Sitting Bull's three granddaughters and his great nephew, a care-worn but dignified Sioux whose name was Clarence Grey Eagle, were somewhere around Mobridge, but not at the tribal council meeting as nearly as we could determine. The group that gathered together Saturday morning in a private residence in Mobridge consisted of eight or ten Sioux, four or five white friends and two newspaper men from Des Moines. The Sioux understood English, but the meeting was conducted in their language with translations for outsiders.

We were there to present our case and ask for the cooperation of the council. Were we to say anything, we were instructed by our white advisors to follow the council's formal manner of dealing with a problem — and were warned to speak respectfully. We sat and listened, but our request was not discussed. Unable to determine the course of the dialogue, it seemed a few words about our mission would be helpful. During one of the many moments of silence, I slowly arose. Gaining the attention of the tribal leaders, I spoke carefully and metaphorically.

We were friends who had flown to the Dakotas from the land of the "Ioway" in a yellow-winged bird, I began. We knew of their effort to right the injustice done when the United States authorities buried Sitting Bull in a military compound in North Dakota, far from the land that had been his as a young man. We wanted to return to Iowa quickly in our yellow bird. From our home in Iowa, we would immediately send their message to the rest of the world. Our story and photographs would tell the world of the success of the family of Sitting Bull. To do this properly, we needed members of the family at the grave site. Our return flight would be made immediately after photographs were taken.

The impression my halting speech made was difficult to determine. There was silence, some subdued conversation, and we were told by white men with us that we should drive to the grave site.

Sitting Bull's bones had been reburied on a treeless bluff overlooking the Missouri River. A somber, overcast day matched the seriousness of the occasion. The three granddaughters and the great nephew of Sitting Bull were brought to the gravesite. Wearing winter coats—dark, simple, and worn—silently they moved behind the new mound of earth covered with fresh lilies. To my surprise, a number of spectators had gathered; large cameras carried by two or three indicated some local papers were represented. My hope for an exclusive photograph was gone.

At my request, made by gestures while readying my Speed Graphic, the Sioux changed their position once or twice as I tried to include the Missouri River and the rolling grass bluffs in the background. The cameras behind me and to my side continued to capture each of my photographs. Within a few minutes the picture taking was completed. The other photographers, in answer to my direct question, indicated they were satisfied.

With my large camera placed on the ground, I motioned to Clarence Grey Eagle to inform him we were finished with the photography. In his tattered overcoat, his head bowed, he led the three women from the grave—passing directly by my right shoulder. Around my neck hung a 35mm camera, a Leica, pre-set at the proper exposure and at an estimated distance. Two rapid exposures were made as the Indians silently and reverently walked away from the grave—I had hardly brought the camera to my eye.

The second of those two exposures became our page-one photograph in the *Sunday Register.* The gray overcast, the barren hills, and the solemn bearing of the Indians make this a strong storytelling image.

Sitting Bull rests here, 1953. Published in *U.S. Camera Annual* and *Photography Annual* both in 1954, and later in *Holiday* magazine. Also hung in *Subjektive Fotografie* exhibit in Germany. Clarence Grey Eagle, who led the party which removed the remains from North Dakota to South Dakota, solemnly leaves the grave with the famous chief's granddaughters.

Aerial photographs were important, but the basic purpose of the *Register*'s aircraft was to save time and beat newspaper deadlines. In the days before the impact of television the *Register* had a Sunday circulation of more than 500,000. Copies of the papers were sold in every corner of Iowa, and we covered stories with special interest to Iowans everywhere possible—staff coverage, with staff photographers. With the aircraft, a breaking story in Dubuque or Sioux City could be covered with a return to Des Moines early enough to meet first-edition deadlines. The following morning the stories and photographs would be on the doorstep of readers in Dubuque or Sioux City. Newspaper trucks every night of the year brought the *Register* to all of Iowa.

Thus, the use of the airplane was simply fast transportation, with the role of aerial photographer important but secondary. Because we had the ability to reach out a distance otherwise impossible, the stories and photographic situations became varied and unlimited.

Even so, a remote Navajo Indian school on the searing floor of Arizona's northern desert was, in July 1953, an unlikely place to find an Iowa reporter-photographer team. The story of two Des Moines Explorer Scouts, lost in the dry washes near the Utah border, was worth the one thousand-mile flight from Iowa.

The Scouts, without food and water for four days, were in serious trouble unless found soon. Authorities, desperate for some sign of their wanderings, only knew the boys had strayed from the group. Lost in this unforgiving wilderness, they had become the focal point for a search that had drawn national attention.

Walter Shotwell, the *Register*'s reporter, flew with me into this unfamiliar territory. We were not certain how close to the search area the aircraft could be put down and decided Winslow, Arizona, would be a good starting place. Flying over the southwestern desert offers, even today, problems not found over Iowa and surrounding states. Piloting a small plane over uninhabitable land calls for equal parts of enthusiasm and caution—with good luck as a welcome addition. Iowa's lush visual feast of green fields, grain elevators, rivers, highways, railroads, and cities is replaced by outcroppings of rock, sandstone promontories, and arroys disappearing into the desert floor, a camouflage reaching to the horizon in all directions.

Shotwell and I hoped to be on the scene when the Scouts were found, but flying the *Register*'s Bonanza into the barren Arizona-Utah desert had special problems. On the fourth day of the rescue effort we took off from Des Moines, and after one enroute refueling stop, touched down lightly on the concrete at Winslow, on the only landing field with a good surface for one hundred miles in any direction, six hours and eight hundred miles from take-off. Our first problem was to find the search team. We wondered if the burning days and chilling nights, the lack of food and water, had already doomed the Scouts.

At Winslow, we learned that Navajo Indians at Window Rock, Arizona, a small Indian community on the New Mexico border, might help us if we flew there. Window Rock, headquarters of the Navajo nation, had an unlighted, unmanned dirt strip for an airport. Despite the need to contact the search team quickly, a landing at Window Rock in the day's fading light—perhaps near darkness—seemed like pushing our luck. After outfitting ourselves with rugged clothing, boots, hats, and gloves we made a dawn take-off from Winslow the next day, arriving early at the Window Rock landing strip. Our caution had been warranted. Paralleling the single dirt runway on the east, a long butte jutted out of the earth joining a rocky cliff on the north, both threats to a night approach by air.

The Navajo at Window Rock were in contact with the search party by shortwave radio. We were lucky; by radio we learned that a lone Navajo, not part of the search party, had happened across strange boot tracks at a place called "No Man Mesa." Another Navajo had tracked the boys across the broken, arid terrain. No longer able to walk, they had collapsed on the desert floor. The morning we arrived at Window Rock, the fifth day of their desert wanderings, the two Scouts had been carried on foot and horseback to Kayenta, an isolated Indian school consisting of a small, one-story structure, a community not on my aeronautical chart. A tiny speck in a trackless area bigger than many of our states, Kayenta was our new goal. Following Navajo advice, we flew generally northwest toward the four-corners wilderness where Arizona, New Mexico, Utah, and Colorado meet. Beyond Kayenta lay thousands of square miles of arid Utah wasteland. The aircraft fuel supply, six hours maximum, was our best assurance for a safe return should we not find the Indian school.

The Navajo told us to fly beyond the north end of Black Mesa, an undefined bulge on the western horizon, and shortly thereafter, below and to the right, we should sight a small cluster of buildings—the Kayenta Indian school. The awesome Canyon de Chelly would be far to the right of our flight track. The vaguely framed Black Mesa and the distant Canyon de Chelly were as difficult to identify as Kayenta promised to be. Shotwell, thirty years later in a *Register* review of this rescue effort, wrote, "It was impossible to find words to describe how remote and dangerous the area was."

The shadow of a Civil Air Patrol plane parked on the desert below, near a level spot in the sand, caught our eyes. With care, a landing could be attempted. The Kayenta Indian school, blending into the desert, was a half-mile north. Circling carefully, we noticed a bulldozer at the edge of the strip. After putting down, we learned that this bulldozer leveled this narrow ribbon in the sand only two days earlier. Civil Air Patrol volunteer aircraft had been flown in to give the search team a special pair of eyes.

We arrived at Kayenta's small Indian schoolhouse within minutes of the time the two Des Moines boys were brought back from their desert ordeal. After five days of searing heat and four cold nights, water from a bug-infested pool and no food, they survived. On foot and horseback, the Navajo returned the Scouts to Kayenta. Worn and hollow-eyed, wearing straw cowboy hats and blue-denim clothing, they were surprisingly alert, able to talk about their experiences, thoughtful while eating their first meal in five days. Subdued by the ordeal, the younger and smaller boy allowed his older companion to speak for both of them; the older boy somberly spoke of their efforts to return to their campsite, and the doubts they had about being found.

A Speed Graphic and a Leica IIIc with a moderately wide angle lens were my cameras on this story. Thirty-five millimeter cameras were still not standard fare for newspaper photographers in 1953, but I was learning to like the naturalness and intimacy the camera produced. The rangefinder Leica was ideal for use in the quiet atmosphere of the Navajo schoolroom. Talking in low, subdued tones, the two survivors were undisturbed by my movements or the whisper of the Leica shutter. Unobtrusively, I took a series of candid photographs capturing the seriousness and relief on their faces. Their expressions as they reviewed their five terrible days, their physical appearance, and the open light in the school room made wonderful, revealing images.

Once refreshed, the boys were taken to the landing strip. There I took photographs as they were secured in a small Civil Air Patrol airplane for a flight to a hospital and a reunion with their parents.

Before our work for the day was finished, the usual first edition deadline had to be met—even though Des Moines was five states away.

Desert rescue, 1953. Exhausted after four days in the
searing Utah-Arizona desert, and taken to the remote
Kayenta Indian school, the two Scouts ponder the near
disaster after their rescue by a lone Navajo.

Lifting off the desert sand at Kayenta, we flew directly to Gallup, New Mexico, to refuel and soon were winging our way southwest to Phoenix over the heavily forested Sierra Ancha mountains of central Arizona. In Phoenix, with film processed and prints made, wirephotos were sent to Des Moines and the deadline met. It had been a full day's work.

Shotwell and I had anticipated a desert tragedy; we were surprised and pleased to cover a story about two Explorer Scouts, far from Iowa, whose luck and recuperative powers were remarkable. A dramatic story with a happy ending. Thirty years later I returned to Kayenta on a highway not in existence in 1953. Still dominated by the desolate, arid terrain of the great American Desert, Kayenta had grown to a population of fifteen hundred. Accommodations had changed. Thirty years later Kayenta had a Holiday Inn!

Journalism and the Unobtrusive Camera *Gallery III*

Storytelling aerial photographs aside, combining the use of 35mm cameras with a changing concept regarding authenticity and realism in photojournalism became a major force in my photographic work during the 1950s. The following photographs include a number of images resulting from an unobtrusive camera and represent the slice of life approach to photojournalism that gained my interest in the post-war years.

Ike and Adlai, presidential campaigners, 1952.

Eisenhower and Minnesota farm wife, 1952.

A pensive moment, 1952.

Ike with Iowans at Abilene, Kansas, 1952.

Nixon, the campaigner, 1958.

Truman at Offutt Air Force Base, Omaha (Strategic Air Command), 1952, and whistle stopping during that year's presidential campaign.

(ABOVE) Ezra Benson, secretary of agriculture in Eisenhower's cabinet, and son, 1954. (BELOW) Alben W. Barkley, vice president in the Truman administration, 1950.

Leon Henderson, World War II price-control czar, 1942.

Jimmy Hoffa, 1957.

A millionaire deals, 1948. *Life* stated: "Always in work clothes, Millionaire Schultz plays pinochle in Happy Jack's tavern when he's not giving away his property." Retired farmer Herman Schultz, 75, gained national prominence when he gave away farm land and eventually was robbed of a large amount of cash.

Scooping the loop, 1953.

Looking, 1953.

His seven died here, 1948. Seven family members, all
children, lie in the smoldering farmhouse ruins.

An indifferent killer, 1953. Fred McManus, captured in Dubuque, Iowa, after a killing spree across many states, offers tenderness to his girlfriend while responding to questions about the trail of five deaths from New York to Iowa.

Polio hit eleven of fourteen in this family. A lead story in
Collier's, November 29, 1952.

Children's despair, 1942. A gusty wind tears their kites
just before the first flight.

Wilt Chamberlain, undergraduate at Kansas University,
1956.

Blind shotputter, Drake Relays, 1954.

Bill Bryson, baseball writer for the *Des Moines Register,*
1954.

High school wrestling, 1955. The *Register*'s caption: HE
lost — but SHE suffered the most.

Smalltown career girl, 1954.

Little Theater leading lady, Claiborne Leachman Cary,
1954.

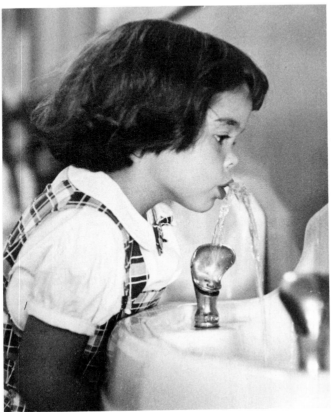

First day at Hillis kindergarten, 1952.

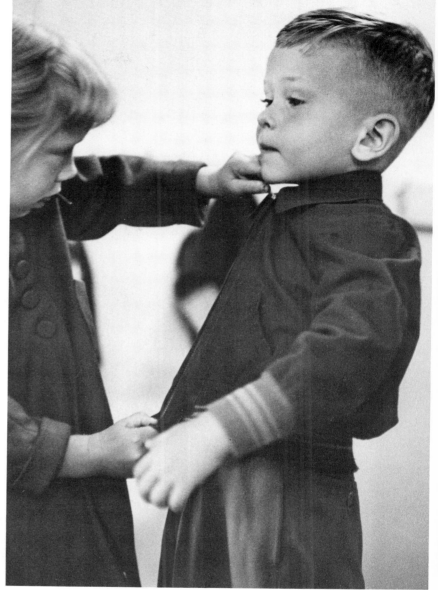

Confronting Santa, 1953.

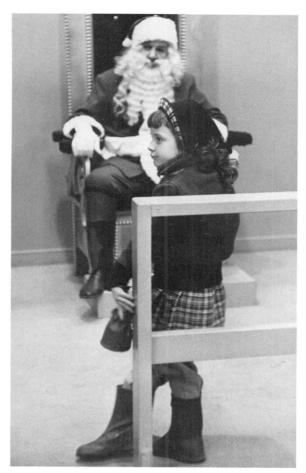

Shenandoah singers; mother and children reunited
Christmas eve, 1954.

The eye, 1951.

Raccoons, 1952.

Two little girls on the dimly lighted sidewalks in a business section of Columbus, Ohio—sisters dressed in identical white organdy—skip in an imaginary circle while their father window shops. Not newsworthy, but much more than that. This scene of innocence and joy reached into my mind and my own life experiences as I struggled to capture its fleeting delightfulness. This visually simple form offers a feeling about the image that is more important than the image itself.

The following images do not represent photojournalism directly, but they are included in the next section as "lasting moments" as defined by Marc Riboud, and they are favorites of mine.

Columbus, Ohio, 1952.

Loras black, 1954.

Two Passionists, 1954.

Priests and kite, 1956.

Man and mud, Floyd River, 1953.

Library man, 1942.

Amana lady, 1953.

Farmer, 1956.

Outburst, 1953. Top honors (Sequence Category) in
University of Missouri School of Journalism and National
Press Photographers' Association Great Pictures
competition, 1953. Also, *Photography Annual 1955*.

Nancy, 1953. *Photography Annual 1954*.

Gamins, 1953.

Ralf Harolde of Hollywood, 1954.

Schoolyard ballet, 1953.

Iowa Falls, 1953. Two a.m. at the railroad station.

Ballet dancers, 1953. *Photography Annual 1954.*

The critics, 1954.

Chicago loop, 1952.

Machinist, 1942.

Curtiss pusher and jet (F-80), 1956.

Endnote

Photographs can reach into our personal lives, perhaps into our memories of childhood, create a mood, suggest a feeling, or offer a reminder of times past. These photographs may inform or engage us artistically, but the appeal reaches further. The response of the photographer to the scene carries into the print itself. Such photography represents a fleeting slice of life, once experienced not to be forgotten, calling us back to earlier years. This intimate glimpse of the passing scene is a moment from the lives of others making a connection with our own. Not needing powerful action or heroic implications, it is the stuff of little moments clinging in our memory, sometimes recalled only vaguely, returning something to our lives. The photograph becomes a catalyst bringing us all together in a common experience. Such photographs make a connection between our imagination and reality—a sense of universality prevails.

A suggestion of the personal connection photographs can leave with our lives was expressed in broader terms by the noted British historian of photography, Helmut Gernsheim. "The most important contribution of photography as an art form lies in its unique ability to chronicle life. . . . it links the family of man. We [viewers] are affected according to the degree of sympathy of the photographer and his (or her) ability to communicate it. No other creative field has such a wonderful task, and offers such unique possibilities as photography."

Index

Aasgaard, M. A., 9
Abercrombie, Thomas, 118
Abilene, Kans., 137
Adams, Ansel, xiii
Adel, Iowa, xii
Air Force, U.S., 45, 92
Allison, Fran, 36, 37
Amana, Iowa, 172
American Magazine, xi, 117, 188
Amerika, 63, 68
Amish, 8
Anderson, Dr. Eddie, xii, 8, 24
Ann Arbor, Mich., 110
Arizona, 47, 126, 127, 129, 130
Army, U.S., 123
Army Air Corps, U.S., 45
Atlanta, Ga., 111

Barkley, Alben W., 140
Beechcraft Bonanza, 47, 91, 100, 109, 126
Benson, Ezra, 140
Big Eight, 109
Big Ten, 8, 109, 110
Black Mesa, 127
Boy Scouts, 47, 126–30
Bright, Johnny, 105, 111–16
Bryson, Bill, 153
Burke, Mary, 6
Burlington, Iowa, 34

Canyon de Chelly, 127
Cartier-Bresson, Henri, xiii, 93, 117, 118, 119
Cary, Claiborne Leachman, 31, 156
Cedar Rapids, Iowa, 7, 8, 9, 15
Cedar Rapids Gazette, xiii, 6, 8, 9

Chamberlain, Wilt, 151
Chicago, Ill., 110, 184
Churchill, Winston, xi, 104, 105, 107
Civil Air Patrol, 128
Civilian Conservation Corps, 3
Civilian Pilot Training, 43, 46
Clutier, Iowa, 26
Collier's, 117, 148, 188
Colorado, 127
Columbus, Ohio, 110, 165, 166
Conger, Dean, 118
Coronet, 188
Craig, Knox, 123
Cummins, Tait, 8
Curtiss pusher, 186

Daily Iowan, 6
Darge, Ron, xiv
Davenport, Iowa, 46
Davenport Times, 6
Decisive Moment, The (Cartier-Bresson), xiii
Dempsey, Jack, 5, 108
Denver Post, 118
Des Moines, Iowa, 4, 12, 16, 32, 45, 46
Des Moines Register and *Tribune,* xii, xiii, 6, 9, 54, 100, 101, 103, 188
Des Moines River, 47, 54
Detroit Times, 54, 55, 188
Drake University, 45, 108, 111–16, 152
Dubuque, Iowa, 126, 147
Dufaycolor, 7

Edmonton Journal, 116

Eisenhower, Dwight D., 3, 132, 134, 136, 137
Eisenstaedt, Alfred E., 8, 105, 118, 119
Encyclopaedia Britannica, 70
Exact Instant, The, 48, 51, 66
Eyemo (Bell and Howell), 109, 112

Felsen, Henry, xi
Floods, 66, 67, 69, 70, 71, 99
Floyd River, 170
Flying Farmers, 47
Folmer-Graflex, 9
Fordham University, 108
Fort Des Moines, Iowa, 46
Fort Dodge, Iowa, 4, 5
Fort Madison, Iowa, xiii
Fort Randall, S.Dak., 68
Fortune, 117, 188
Fort Wayne, Ind., 111
Fort Yates, N.Dak., 123
Franco, General, xii
Fulton, Mo., 104, 105

Gallup, N.Mex., 130
Gartner, Carl, 43
Georgia Tech, 111
Gernsheim, Helmut, 187
Gilka, Robert, 118
Gladstone, Iowa, 3
Godowsky, Leopold, 7
Good News VIII and *IX,* 100
Graflex, 93
Grange, Red, 108
Grapes of Wrath, The (Steinbeck), 3
Great Pictures, 70, 174, 188
Grey Eagle, Clarence, 123–25

Hardendorf, Roy, 8
Hardy, Arnold, 111
Harolde, Ralf, 178
Henderson, Leon, 141
Hoffa, Jimmy, 142
Holiday, 117, 125, 188

Humeston, Iowa, 35
Hunter, Dan, 8

Illinois, 88
Independence, Mo., 8
Iowa City, Iowa, 6, 8, 14
Iowa Falls, Iowa, 180
Iron Curtain, xi, 104, 105
Ironmen, 8, 24
Iwasaki, Carl, 118
Iwo Jima, 111

Jones, Bobby, 108

Kalona, Iowa, 8
Kauffman, Mark, 70
Kayenta, Ariz., 127–30
Kent State University, 55
Kinnick, Nile, xii, 8, 24
Kodachrome, 7
Kodak, Eastman, 7

Lake Mills Graphic, 9
Leachman, Cloris, 30
Leica, 6, 7, 120, 124, 128
Life, 8, 47, 50, 51, 52, 54, 58, 63, 67, 70, 99, 104, 111, 115, 117, 118, 120, 121, 122, 143, 188
Lincoln Highway, 3
Lindbergh, Charles A., 4, 9
Little Theater (Des Moines), xiii, 156
Lone Tree, Iowa, 85
Look, 117

MacDonald, Kenneth, 46
McManus, Fred, 147
Magnum Photo Group, 117
Maloney, Tom, 56, 72, 75
Mannes, Leopold, 7
Marshall, Verne, 9
Mason City Globe-Gazette, 112

Millen, Cliff, 105
Miller, Merle, 6
Mills, George, 105
Milwaukee Journal, 118
Mississippi River, 83, 94
Missouri River, 47, 66, 68, 70, 99, 124
Missouri Valley Conference, 108, 111
Mobridge, S.Dak., 123
Modern Photography, 118
Moline, Ill., 46
Montana, 47
Monterrey, Mexico, 47
Mott, Frank Luther, 6, 8
Museum of Modern Art (New York, N.Y.), 48, 51, 66, 188

National Geographic, 118
National Press Photographers' Association, 174, 188
National Recovery Act, 3
Navajo, 126–29
Navy, U.S., 43–46, 56, 91
New Mexico, 127
New Yorker, The, 101
New York Times, 111
Nishnabotna River, 67, 71
Nixon, Richard, 138
North Dakota, 124
Notre Dame University, 108, 109
Numa, Iowa, 104

Ohio State University, 109, 110
Oklahoma A&M (Oklahoma State University), 112–15
Old Capitol (Iowa City, Iowa), 8, 14, 24
Oldfield, Barney, 108
Olshwager, Ron, 111
Omaha, Nebr., 89, 120, 122
Omaha World-Herald, 6
Ottosen, Iowa, 104

Pageant, 117, 188

Pearl Harbor, 12
Phoenix, Ariz., 130
Photography Annual, 48, 72, 75, 122, 125, 174, 176, 182, 188
Photo-Secession group, xiii
Pittsburgh, Pa., 47
Plain Speaking (Miller), 6
Pulitzer Prize, 47, 104, 108, 110, 111, 115, 188

Quill, The, 119

Read, Iowa, 81
Retina, Kodak, 6, 7
Riboud, Marc, 117, 165
Rio Grande, 47
Robinson, John, 111–15
Rock Island, Ill., 46
Rockne, Knute, 108
Rolleicord, 7
Rolleiflex, 7
Roosevelt, Franklin D., 6
Rosenthal, Joe, 110
Rural Electrification Administration, 4
Ruth, Babe, 108

Saarbrucken, West Germany, 51
Schau, Virginia, 111
Schultz, Herman, 143
Scottish Highlanders, xi
Scully, Julia, 118
Shenandoah, Iowa, 162
Sherwood, Bob, 6
Shotwell, Walter, 126, 128, 130
Sioux City, Iowa, 126
Sitting Bull, 123–25
Smith, W. Eugene, 105, 118
Sochurek, Howard, 118
South Dakota, 48, 50, 63, 68, 78, 84, 95, 123, 125
Speed Graphic, 9, 56, 57, 59, 93, 103, 104, 109, 116, 117, 118, 124, 128

Spiegel, Bob, 112, 113
Spirit of St. Louis, 4
Steichen, Edward, 48, 66, 119, 188
Steinbeck, John, 3
Stevenson, Adlai E., 132
Stieglitz, Alfred, xiii, 116
Stillwater, Okla., 47, 104, 111, 112
Strategic Air Command, 92, 139
Subjektive Fotografie, 51, 125
Swift, Globe, 47, 100

Tilden, Bill, 108
Time, 188
Truman, Harry S., 8, 46, 105, 139
Truro, Iowa, 23
Tubbs, Irl, 24
Tubbs, Sally, 24
Tunney, Gene, 5, 108

University of Iowa, xii, 6, 8, 24, 110
University of Michigan, 110
University of Missouri, 8, 70, 99,
    174, 188

University of Pittsburgh, 110
U.S. Camera Annual, 48, 53, 56, 68,
    72, 75, 99, 115, 121, 122, 125,
    188
USS *Monitor,* 5
Utah, 126, 127, 129

Waterloo, Iowa, 36, 37
Westminster College, 105
White, Maury, 111, 116
Wills, Helen, 108
Window Rock, Ariz., 127
Winecoff Hotel, 111
Winner, S.Dak., 84
Winslow, Ariz., 126, 127
Wiota, Iowa, 26
Wisconsin State Journal, 112
Women's Auxiliary Corps, 46
Women's Home Companion, 117, 188
Works Progress Administration, 3
Wright, Frank Lloyd, 119

Yates, George, 9

About the author

In 1958, at the age of forty-one, photojournalist Don Ultang left the staff of the *Des Moines Register* to pursue a business career. He left behind a body of photographic work that stands among the best of the era. Ultang's photographs in the years 1940–1958 appeared not only in the *Register; American Magazine, Collier's, Fortune, Coronet, Time, Pageant, Woman's Home Companion, Holiday,* and *Life* magazine all featured his work.

The *Life* photographs in particular brought Don Ultang to national attention. Beginning in 1949, the young photographer received a string of awards, including a *Detroit Times* feature award (1949), a University of Missouri-National Press Photographers "Great Pictures" award (1951), a Pulitzer Prize for News Photography (1952), a portfolio in *U.S. Camera Annual* (1954), a selection as a Photographer of the Year by *Photography Annual,* and a second "Great Pictures" prize (1954). His photographs were chosen by Edward Steichen for exhibition at New York's Museum of Modern Art (1949) and were later exhibited in Germany as well.

Today Don Ultang lives in Des Moines with his wife, Elizabeth Kasten-Ultang. The Ultangs travel extensively, spending time each year in New Mexico and on Nantucket Island. Ultang's photographs are exhibited in Iowa and throughout the United States.